THE

SERPENT

AND THE

RED

THREAD

THE DEFINITIVE BIOGRAPHY OF EVIL

THE
SERPENT
AND THE
RED
THREAD

THE DEFINITIVE BIOGRAPHY OF EVIL

by Diane Weber Bederman

mantua books

2019

PRAISE FOR THE SERPENT AND THE RED THREAD

Diane Weber Bederman is very passionate in understanding the evil mindset behind hatred against Jews. Her book 'The Serpent and The Red Thread' is a sort of short history of historic incidences related to this evil mindset. This book may provide a reference to our present day world leadership in terms of curbing this hatred. Dealing with controversial and messy religious and political history is not an easy task. Holocaust denial and growing antisemitism can never be addressed precisely without addressing the root causes of these hateful attitudes.

— Tahir Aslam Goram, Television
producer and author

Poetic, mystical, and prophetic, 'The Serpent and the Red Thread' is a unique, unflinching look at the history of Jew-hatred from Biblical-era persecution through the Holocaust to today's Muslim Brother-hood. It is an essential reminder that the Jewish people have always been stalked by evil, and yet always prevail.

— Mark Tapson, Shillman Fellow at the
David Horowitz Freedom Center and
author of Chivalry and the War on Men

It is quite an achievement. It's the kind of project--terrifying, daunting--that most writers wouldn't even contemplate, let alone carry through--and you did it with style and power. It is riveting.

— Janice Fiamengo, Professor of English at
the University of Ottawa

Drawing upon history and characters like Abraham, Sarah, Isaac, Jesus, Paul and 'hitler', Bederman lays bare the human dichotomy between good and evil, and love and hate. Exposing the tug-of-war within the human soul and influenced by cultural impact, this book provides a creative, enlightening and much needed crash course in human responsibility. The Serpent renders an inescapable call to confront one's deeper consciousness and the question to one's self: can one remain neutral and in denial in the face of egregious evil without bearing a degree of culpability? as witnessed in the Holocaust.

— Christine Douglass-Williams, International award-winning journalist and best-selling author of *The Challenge of Modernizing Islam*

From humanity's first encounter with evil up until our present time, author Diane Weber Bederman lays out the unparalleled, irrational hate of the Jewish people. With often chilling prose, she takes us down the historical paths of nations, religions and ideologies to uncover the webs that trapped and devoured the people who gifted the world with compassion and ethics. Citing often unfamiliar sources, the author unravels the thread of hate that ran through primitive times yet also through the likes of the Enlightenment. It was the progression birthed in the Enlightenment that promised to better society, It was the same progression that set the stage for the unparalleled and unprecedented pinnacle of enmity—the Holocaust.

Passionate, personal, and presenting the facts, this is much more than a book. It is an indictment on a world that has forgotten that the mass industrial murder of 6 million Jews on Europe's soil was done in the name of culture and progression. It is a cry from the heart, a warning. The serpent of antisemitism has never been apprehended. It is on the loose again and it's ravenous for Jews. Today it leashes it's venom at the Jewish homeland. The author burdens us with the freedom of choice. Whoever we are, we have a moral duty to combat this hate that in living memory saw to the annihilation of millions of human beings in the name of progression.

— Kay Wilson, Author of *The Rage Less Traveled*

'The Serpent and the Red Thread' chronicles the miasmal hatred, pogroms, and ruthless antisemitism that continues to persecute the Jewish people today. Bederman manages to bring beauty to this

horror, which makes her book an engrossing read for students and scholars alike.

Diane Weber Bederman offers the reader a fascinating documentary of antisemitism and its inspiration from ancient times until today. Bederman deftly follows the red thread of antisemitism that begins in the Garden of Eden, threads its way through the descendants of Amalek, Adolph Hitler, and finally into the 21st century where Islamic Jew hatred is Hitlerian in intensity. Antisemitism has managed to wend its way through time and civilizations in its inexhaustible efforts to destroy the Jewish people. The torch of antisemitism passes from generation to generation by leaders who look to history to rationalize their savagery.

— Linda Goudsmit, Author of *Dear America: Who's Driving the Bus?* and children's series *Mimi's STRATEGY*

It has been called the oldest and the longest hatred. It has persisted through the millennia making its way through human history from Antiquity to Modernity. As such, it has been directed at a small group of people within a sea of vast multitude of people and singled it out for deprecation, persecution, and attempts at annihilation. Much ink has been spilled to account for, to explain and even justify and legitimize this phenomenon. Why the Jews? Is the puzzling question to which there is no plausible answer except for those who carry this evil in their hearts.

Evil is the answer to be found in the small volume by Diane Weber Bederman which she titled 'The Serpent and the Red Thread.' Evil, she explains, has beset the world since the beginning of time—which in this version is associated with the Creation as described in the Hebrew Bible and the Garden of Eden. The beautiful parable of the serpent planting the seed of evil in the heart of the first humans highlights the eternal battle against the good. More often than not, it is the force of evil that seems to win out over a more benevolent inclination. The ultimate form of Evil finds its expression in the form of hatred of the Jews, or antisemitism in a modern-day coinage. The author takes the reader on the winding trail this Evil take in its variant forms—religious intolerance to cultural calumny formulated in Christian Church doctrine and the race theories that sprouted from the secularized modern era on and reached its culmination, its ultimate explosion under the Nazi regime.

As the author weaves and spins out this thread—the Red Thread of Evil, she calls it in a felicitous metaphor—she gathers together an enormous amount of material that documents the poison spread by even some of greatest and most admired thinkers to the venom spewed by the evil incarnate in the person of Adolf Hitler. She takes the reader on a journey, a trail of tears and suffering experienced by few other groups. Yet, even after the most catastrophic event of the Nazi murder of millions, the evil of antisemitism that has hounded and pursuit the Jewish people is not extinguish. In fact, in recent years it has gathered strength and its poison has been spreading like an epidemic in the Middle East, where the Jews regained their ancient homeland, Europe, and even America. As the author states, the Red Thread of Evil has found yet another home in the hands of another group, the followers of the religion of Allah, who are intent on accomplishing what no other regime or culture had been able to do: to wipe the Jews off the face of the earth. Alarmingly, they have found many in the West who make themselves willing accomplices in the campaign of lies and distortions against Israel and the Jewish people elsewhere.

This latter-day incarnation of Evil frequently finds accomplices among young people, uneducated and uninformed and easily taken in by extremist diatribes. That is why it is so important that this small volume with its treasure of information presented in a readable, even gripping narrative is placed into the hands of a wider public, but most especially impressionable youths in universities and high schools. A timely document that will enlighten those receptive to thought and the truth.

— Brigitte M Goldstein, Ph.D., historical novelist

Published by: Mantua Books Ltd.
Canada
www.mantuabooks.com
Email: administration@mantuabooks.com

Library and Archives Canada Cataloging in Publication

Title: The serpent and the red thread : the definitive biography of evil / Diane Weber Bederman.
Names: Bederman, Diane Weber, author.
Identifiers: Canadiana 20190216794 | ISBN 9781927618134 (softcover)
Subjects: LCSH: Antisemitism—History.
Classification: LCC DS145 .B34 2019 | DDC 305.892/4—dc23

Cover Illustration and design by Barbara Jensen

To my father Abraham and my mother Sarah; to my children and grandchildren and all who follow; and always, Marc

CONTENTS

Contents

Memory is the scribe of the soul

~ Aristotle

PREFACE

This is a book, a documentary, about the oldest, most irrational evil: Jew hatred; told through the voices of Biblical and historical figures. I want to take you on a journey through time, sharing the presence of history and our collective memories, beginning where all time begins: The Garden of Eden, where we meet the serpent who has in his mouth the red thread which he takes with him as it connects evil through time. I have chosen to incorporate the Chinese literary device, the red thread, to connect the most evil of humankind, the Amaleks of history. The ones who spread irrational hate.

All of the events I report are historical, factual, sometimes shared through the stories of my characters: Abraham, Sarah, Isaac, Jesus, Paul and hitler. One need not be a student of the bible or history to follow the travels of the red thread woven by the serpent from the Garden.

In the Story of Elie, I have taken liberally from the stories told by Elie Weisel. The Story of Sophia is based on the book *The Holocaust by Bullets: A Priest's Journey to Uncover the Truth Behind the Murder of 1.5 Million Jews* by Father Patrick Desbois.

I learned much from Elaine Pagel's writings as well as Lucy S. Dawidowicz, from her books.

You may hear echoes from:

- Deborah Lipstadt; The Eichman Trial; Nextbook; Schocken New York 2011
- Nicholas Goodrick-Clarke; The Occult Roots of Nazism: Secret Aryan Cults and their influence on Nazi Ideology; New York University Press 1985/1992
- The words spoken by adolf hitler (1889–1945) are mostly his own, although I have taken the liberty of assigning statements made by his compatriots to him. I write his name with a lower case "h" because no respect must ever be accorded to him.

- Islamophobia in Nazi Germany comes from https://www.wilsonquarterly.com/quarterly/fall-2014-the-great-wars/
- The musical composition by Olivier Messiaen (1908–1992) Quatuor pour la fin du temps (Quartet for the end of time) was first played in 1941 by prisoners at a Nazi POW camp. I have taken that story and moved it to a different time and place during WWII.
- Dance Me to the End of Love: lyrics by Leonard Cohen
- The story of Wotan comes from the writings of Carl Jung (1875–1961).
- For those of you well versed in the Bible, a great deal of dialogue will be familiar to you.
- And a thank you to J.K. Rawlings, for introducing me to her fictional character, Voldemort, in the Harry Potter series.
- Some of Louis Farrakhan's comments come from https://www.jewishvirtuallibrary.org/minister-louis-farrakhan-in-his-own-words
- The Dream in Chapter 18 comes from Palestine Media Watch [Zayzafuna, February 2011]
- http://www.palwatch.org/main.aspx?fi=157&doc_id=26539
- The Al Fatiha prayer, to which I refer in Chapter 18, is sourced from American Center for Democracy. http://acdemocracy.org/what-are-praying-muslims-repeating-17-times-daily/?fbclid=IwAR3ZEeoIKN5gaFktiWp-3GVWnurbuxfloTsHt4nA6rP6mWw-yWb88Lx8OxU

When I finished the manuscript and added numbers to the chapters, I realized that the book consisted of eighteen chapters. The number 18 in Hebrew means Life.

The death of so many Jews led to a great loss to their collective culture. So much of their music, symphonies, poetry, prose, art-work, and stories died with them and the children never to be born.

INTRODUCTION

A hard lot has been created for human beings
A heavy yoke lies on the children of Adam
From the day they come out of their mother's womb,
To the day they return to the mother of them all.
What fills them with foreboding and their hearts with fear is
dread of the day of death

~ Ecclesiasticus 40:1

What would the teachers of Christianity say if they had been present during the Holocaust? How would the mother and father of the Jewish people, Abraham and Sarah, and their only son, Isaac, respond to the attempted destruction of all of their children? How would hitler have justified his actions?

The Shoah (Holocaust) is the ultimate account of evil. There is no other historical epoch so malevolent, so intent on wiping out a people, not for something they had done, but simply for being. There have been other attempts—but none so well-planned nor permitted by all the nations of the world.

What freezes the blood in one's veins is the knowledge that the extermination of a people 3500 years old was calmly and meticulously planned over a period of time while the world watched.

In 1933 hitler clearly said "Why does the world shed crocodile's tears over the richly merited fate of a small Jewish minority? . . .I ask Roosevelt, I ask the American people: Are you prepared to receive in your midst these well-poisoners of the German people and the universal spirit of Christianity? We would willingly give every one of them a free steamer-ticket and a thousand-mark note for travelling expenses, if we could get rid of them."

In 1938, hitler once again made his intentions known in Nuremburg, without ambiguity. He commented, *inter alia*, on what he perceived as the self-righteous and hypocritical attitude of the democratic countries toward the plight of Jews under German control:

"They complain...of the boundless cruelty with which Germany—and now Italy also—seek to rid themselves of their Jewish elements. All these great democratic empires taken together have only a handful of people to the square kilometre. Both in Italy and Germany there are over 140. Yet formerly Germany, without blinking an eyelid, for whole decades admitted these Jews by the hundred thousand. But now...when the nation is no longer willing to be sucked dry by these parasites, on every side one hears nothing but laments. But lamentations have not led these democratic countries to substitute helpful activity at last for their hypocritical questions; on the contrary, these countries with icy coldness assured us that obviously there was no place for the Jews in their territory...So no help is given, but morality is saved."

Heinrich Himmler (1900–1945), leader of the SS, had built the organization from 280 persons in 1929, to nearly a quarter million people by 1934. It was the SS that would be responsible for annihilating the Jews. In 1935, a separate Jewish affairs desk was established. Leopold von Mildenstein (1902–1968) was in charge, and he hired Adolph Eichmann (1906–1962) as his expert on Zionism. In 1935, an entire bureaucracy was established to gather data on the Jews at home and abroad. No detail was too small.

Himmler was also Chief of the German Police and, on November 25, 1939, in full accord with hitler, he said: "We won't waste much time on the Jews. It's great to get to grips with the Jewish race at last. The more they die the better...We want to put half to three-quarters of all Jews east of the Vistula. We will crush these Jews wherever we can...Get the Jews out of the Reich...We have no use for Jews in the Reich. Probably the line of the Vistula, behind this line no more. We are the most important people here..."

For far too many countries, when it came to the Jews; none is too many.

જી

Who shall live? And who shall die.
And who by fire? Who by water?

Who by sword? And who by beast?
Who by hunger? And who by thirst?
Who by strangling? And who by stoning?
Who in the sunshine? Who in the night time?
Who by high ordeal? Who by common trial?
Who by very slow decay?
And who shall I say is calling?
And who by brave assent? Who by accident?
Who by solitude? Who by his own hand?
Who in mortal chains? Who in power?
Who should I say is calling?

~ Leonard Cohen / Unetaneh Tokef

1

EVIL ALWAYS TRIES TO KILL THE MESSENGER OF COMPASSION

> *Love and compassion are necessities, not luxuries. Without them humanity cannot survive.*
>
> ~ Dalai Lama

There is an ancient Chinese proverb which states: "An invisible thread connects those who are destined to meet, regardless of time, place, and circumstance. The thread may stretch or tangle. But it will never break."

This is the story of a particularly dangerous red thread that invisibly connects evil from one generation to the next. It begins in the Garden of Eden where all things begin. On the sixth day, God created man and woman: not from an utterance, not from a word, but from His hands and His breath; we are created in His image, capable of reason, moral thinking, and free will. He created Adam and Eve, the first children, the first of His children. And He placed them in the lush Garden of Eden. And He told them to eat and enjoy all that was before them in the Garden of Eden, all but the fruit of the Tree of Knowledge of Good and Evil. That tree—right there in the middle of the garden. That sensual tree with luscious fruit. That tree. Don't eat from that tree.

How could they not try the fruit? It's not as if it were hidden in a corner of the garden behind a fence. It was right there. In front of them. So easy to access. So forbidden. It is too much to bear. And the serpent, so sweet and so smooth of speech told Eve to take of the fruit. And Eve, ever so human, forgot, or chose to forget, the admonishment against eating that fruit. And Eve, being so human, offered the fruit to Adam and now the two innocent children had to leave the Garden; because of one small error in decision-making. And the serpent watched and waited with the red thread dangling from his mouth.

And that red thread made its way through the descendants of Amalek—leader of the nation who attacked the weakest among the Jewish people as they made their way out of Egypt, after 400 years of slavery, into the desert on their way to the Promised Land.

Amalek; the first, but sadly not the last, of those who carried within them the evil of the serpent. The Red Serpent had within his jaws that first piece of that red thread and that thread stretched, twisted and bent itself to find its way into the hand of hitler, the vilest of all in the chain of Amalek.

And then, against all odds, it threaded its way into the 21st century to once again try to destroy the Jewish people, the people of The Book; the people who gave us the ethic to care for the weak, the sick, the widow, the orphan, the other; who brought into the world the notion that all people have equal intrinsic value; the people who, despite all of the attempts to exterminate them, continue to teach and preach the ethic of compassion.

Perhaps that is the reason. Evil always tries to kill the messenger of compassion.

2

THE SERPENT, THE VOICE OF TEMPTATION

In the face of suffering, one has no right to turn away, not to see. In the face of injustice, one may not look the other way. When someone suffers, and it is not you, he comes first. His very suffering gives him priority. When someone cries and it is not you, he has rights over you.

~ Elie Wiesel

The red serpent, red thread clenched in its jaw, had once again slithered out from the deep, and found a new home. From its beginning in the Garden, the Serpent, the voice of temptation, made its way through time, entering the bodies of those who knew not of compassion, justice, mercy, charity, and loving-kindness. He found a home in Amalek, the one who attacked the weakest of the Israelites, the women, children, and the sick, as they escaped across the desert away from the oppressor, Pharaoh, who had enslaved them in work camps.

Without provocation, Amalek (the leader of the tribe that God said He would utterly blot out of memory under heaven for what they had done to the Jewish people as they fled Egypt), had led its army against the weakest of the people who had just fled from slavery and were walking through the desert toward freedom. It was the same tribe that King Saul battled hundreds of years later but, defying God's command to destroy all of them, men, women, children, and animals, he spared their King, Agag, and with him evil carried on hiding underground only to resurface with Haman, the descendent of Agag. Haman, the one who incited the King of Persia to annihilate the Jews, to wipe them off the face of the earth.

And Haman, persecutor of the Jews, said to his King Ahashverus: "There is one people scattered, yet separate among the nations in all the provinces of your kingdom; and their laws

3

are different from those of every people; while they do not execute the laws of the king; and it is no profit for the king to tolerate them. If it be pleasing to the king, let a decree be written to destroy them."

And the King of Persia replied: "I have resolved never to be carried away by the insolence of power, but always to rule with moderation and clemency, so as to assure my subjects a life ever free from storms and offering my kingdom the benefits of civilization and free transit from end to end, to restore peace which all men desire. We have been informed by one of the eminent among us for prudence and well proved for his unfailing devotion and unshakeable trustworthiness, and in rank second only to our majesty, there is mingled among all the tribes of the earth a certain ill-disposed people, the Jews, opposed by its laws and to every other nation and continually defying the royal ordinances, in such a way as to obstruct that form of government assures to us to the general good. Considering therefore that this people, unique in its kind, is in complete opposition to all humanity from which it differs, by its outlandish laws, that it is hostile to our interests and that it commits the most heinous crimes to the point of endangering the stability of the realm: We command that those persons appointed to watch over our interests to destroy, root and branch, including women and children, without any pity or mercy, so that, these past and present malcontents being in one day forcibly thrown down into Hades, our government may hence forward enjoy perpetual stability and peace."

But the attempt failed. The Jews lived on.

And the serpent slithered forward in time, sniffing the air, looking for willing participants. There were many throughout the millennia. The red thread found a home in Muhammad. Soon after he anointed himself Prophet, he expelled two tribes of Jews: the Banu Qaynuqa in 624 CE and the Nadir in 625 CE. In 627 CE, Muhammad committed an atrocity against the tribe of Banu Qurayza, a peaceful community of farmers, the last remaining major tribe of Jews in Medina. It is reported that more than 800 men and boys, who had surrendered, were brought in batches to trenches that had been dug for them. Forced to stand over the trenches they were then beheaded. In 628 Muhammad conquered Khaybar, murdering the leaders and taking a wife, Saffiya, after beheading her husband Kinana al Rabi of the Bani Nadir.

Words of hate from Muhammad, a man of religion, slipped so easily off his lips; "The last hour would not come unless the Muslims will fight against the Jews and the Muslims would kill them until the Jews would hide themselves behind a stone or a tree and a stone or a tree would say: 'Muslim, or the servant of Allah, there is a Jew behind me; come and kill him;' but the tree Gharqad would not say, for it is the tree of the Jews."

He admonished, "The resurrection of the dead will not arrive until you will fight the Jews and kill them. . ." And his Scriptures spoke of hate for 'the other'. "Jews are among the worst enemies of Islam." This was a man of faith who had beheaded the men and the pubescent boys, enslaved the women and children and seized their wealth. He left the land covered in Jewish blood; a genocide; foretelling another time when Jews would again be sacrificed in trenches.

Today, chants of *Khaybar Khaybar ya Yahoud, jaish Muhammad saufa ya'ud*, meaning "Khaybar, Khaybar, O Jews, the army of Muhammad will return" and the Hezbollah version *Khaybar, Khaybar ya Sahyoun, Hizbullah qadimun*, meaning "Khaybar, Khaybar O Zionists, Hezbollah is coming soon," are shared. Tribalism through time.

The serpent, red thread clenched, moved on, in the time of the universe, between the beginning of time and the end of time it was merely a moment and found a home in Spain, as the Muslim domain fell, and the Catholic world rose. The Inquisition: convert, die, or be expelled. The Inquisition began mid-thirteenth century with the condemning of the Talmud. Thousands of volumes of the book were burned. In 1288 the first mass burning of Jews took place; in France. And spread. In Spain, the red thread found a place to stay in Tomás de Torquemada, the Spanish Amalek Grand Inquisitor, who, under Queen Isabella and King Ferdinand, presided over the death of more than two thousand Jews burned at the stake, auto da fés, in Spain. It is estimated that 32,000 "heretics" were murdered the same way by the time the killing spree in Europe ended.

And then there was quiet. Not that attacks against the Jewish people ended, but they remained sporadic, for the red thread was searching for the perfect leader to carry out the actions of Amalek. And with patience, the thread succeeded. It found its next true home in adolf hitler.

3

THE SCAPEGOAT

National Socialism could not have come to power in Germany if it had not found, in broad strata of the population, soil prepared for its sowing of poison. It is not accurate to say that the high military or the great industrialists alone bear the guilt.

~ Dr. Konrad Adenauer

Over the centuries antisemitism had reared its ugly head in Christian Europe and, by the 1800s, the people in Germany and Austria were bathed in its rhetoric. Memories of Wotan washed over them; memories of greatness. The hatred became especially virulent after World War 1 when a scapegoat was needed to assuage the German humiliation over the loss of the war, the reparations demanded of them, and assist them in their need for self-esteem in a time of political and economic chaos. They chose to blame and then sacrifice "the Jew."

The land had been well-prepared for the seeds of the poisonous vine known as antisemitism, long before the rise of National Socialism. In 1793, Johann Gotlieb Fichte (1762–1814), the father of both German nationalism and German antisemitism, characterized the Jews as a state within a state that would undermine the German nation. The only way in which he could concede giving rights to Jews would be "to cut off all their heads in one night and to sew new ones on their shoulders, which should contain not a single Jewish idea."

This took place in a time of revived German nationalism and a renewal of the mythic Volk. The Volk, more than a people within a nation, it was a group bonded by a transcendental essence, nature, cosmos, and mythos. Each member of the Volk was connected one to the other, in a sense from one soul to another. And so began the new world order based on the concept of Volk. From the lips of Friedrich Ludwig Jahn (1778–1852), "A state without Volk is nothing, a soulless artifice; a Volk without a state is nothing, a bodiless airy phantom, like the Gypsies and the Jews. Only state and Volk can form a Reich, and such a Reich cannot be preserved without Volkdom."

Foreigners could not be allowed to enjoy the rights of real Germans; Christian Germans. The call rang out to convert the Jews to Christianity so they could acquire the true German ethic. The goal: destroy the Jewish people in the land. Christian Friedrich Rühs (1781–1820) wrote, "A foreign people cannot obtain the rights which the Germans enjoy partly through being Christians...Everything should be done to induce the Jews...to accept Christianity and through it to be led to a true acquisition of German ethnic characteristics and thus to effect the destruction of the Jewish people."

In 1819 came cries of "Hep! Hep! Hep!" Death and destruction to all Jews. We must take revenge against the Jews who are living among us and who are increasing like locusts." In the latter half of the 19th century Paul de Lagarde, the Volkist patron saint of the antisemitic movement wrote:

"Every Jew is proof of the enfeeblement of our national life and the worthlessness of what we call the Christian religion." And later "One would need a heart as hard as crocodile hide not to feel sorry for the poor exploited Germans and – which is identical – not to hate the Jews and despise those who – out of humanity! – defend these Jews or who are too cowardly to trample this usurious vermin to death. With trichinae and bacilli one does not negotiate, nor are trichinae and bacilli to be educated; they are to be exterminated as quickly and thoroughly as possible."

This became hitler's war cry.

The Mittelstand—the middle class—small farmers, peasants, artisans and small business men feared the rapidly changing society that was turning forward to industrialization and away from the land. They embraced the "Jewish Conspiracy" rhetoric of

Berliner Adolph Stocker (1835–1909). In 1879 Stocker had shared his views at a Christian Social meeting:

"Modern Jewry is a great danger to German national life. The Jews are a people within a people, a state within a state, a separate tribe within a foreign race who pitted their unbroken Semitic character against Teutonic nature, their rigid cult of law or their hatred of Christians against Christianity."

In universities in the 1880s the cry was heard, "The Jews are our misfortune." In the fall of 1880, the antisemites petition was circulated by two school teachers depicting the Jews as exploitative masters, who would destroy the German fatherland. "Jews are alien people", they said. "Their thinking and feeling are completely alien to the German Volk. If the German people are not to be destroyed and fall into economic slavery by the Jews, steps need to be taken to liberate the German people from this Jewish danger." By the spring of 1881, there were 225,000 signatures, mostly Prussian; 9000 from Bavaria, and 4000 university students.

Antisemitic rhetoric began to lead to attacks against Jews.

More university professors began to sing the same antisemitic song. Eugene Karl Duhring (1833–1921), a philosopher and economist at the University of Berlin wrote *The Jewish Question as a Racial, Moral and Cultural Question* in 1877. He spouted that Germany's social corruption was the consequence of parasitic Jews settling in Germany. He described the Jews as a "counter-race" separated from all humanity, whom neither conversion nor assimilation could affect because their basic nature was evil and unchangeable. He was highly respected amongst his students.

Duhring was idealized by Georg von Schonerer (1842–1921) who formulated Pan-Germanism. Guido von List (1848–1919), another vehement Jew hater was an associate of Schonerer. He contributed to Pan German ideology; "What the Jew believes is all one, in his race lies the swinishness." hitler synthesized the writings and developed a revised Pan-Germanism; one that did not include the Jews.

This hateful antisemitic ideology did not stay within the hallowed hall of higher learning. In the agricultural areas, the peasants advanced the notion that Germany "repeal, by legal means, Jewish emancipation by placing the Jews under alien legislation." Jews were described as an octopus with claws in every sphere of German life. This belief morphed into the description of Jews as "beasts of prey" and "cholera bacilli." In 1892, all the rhetoric and ranting turned the Conservative Party toward anti-semitism as a political tool to win elections. Antisemitism was given the imprimatur of rationality. "We fight the multifarious and obtrusive Jewish influence that decomposes our people's life."

The Agrarian League started its antisemitic output in 1894:

"Jewry has become altogether too mighty in our country and has acquired a decisive say in the press, in trade and on the exchanges."

"Agriculture and Jewry must fight to the death, until one or other lies lifeless—or at least powerless—on the ground."

By the beginning of the 20th century, each year "tens of thousands of antisemitic pamphlets were sent free to all officials of the state and members of the upper ten thousand." They were in every library. By the 1920s, there were approximately 430 antisemitic associations and societies, including the List Society, the Austrian Alpine Association, The German Language Club, the German Social Party, and the Thule Society which spread Volkist racial propaganda which was based on nineteenth century Romanticism; a belief that the true German was spiritually con-nected to the very soil of the homeland, rooted in the ground itself, unlike the wandering materialistic Jew.

Rudolph Hess (1894–1987), one of hitler's closest followers, was a member. There were as many as 700 antisemitic periodicals. Antisemitic bills were introduced into state and national legis-latures. Antisemitism was in the printed word, in speeches, and in music. The air was saturated with hatred of the Jews. hitler discovered the works of Richard Wagner (1813–1883) in the early 1900s. After reading Wagner's prose, *Jews in Music and Decay and*

Regeneration, hitler declared Wagner as great as Frederick the Great and Martin Luther. "Whoever wants to understand National Socialist Germany must know Wagner." Wagner was a strong supporter and promoter of the Volk and Teutonic myths. "Emancipation from the yoke of Judaism appears to be the foremost necessity." Wagner's hatred of the Jews carried forward long after his death.

hitler was also a follower of the writings of Lanz von Liebenfels (1874–1954). He waxed poetic about the struggle between the blonde Aryans (the light), and the dark, hairy ape-men representing the lower races. In the early 1900s, Liebenfels declared "We would never dream of preaching pogroms, because they will come without encouragement." He advocated ridding the world of the Jews, a mongrelized breed.

hitler found the works of his predecessors wanting. The Jewish danger, he said, is based on more than religion; it is based also on racial knowledge. After all, if it is only religion, "If the worst came to worst, a splash of baptismal water could always save the business and the Jew at the same time." To hitler, he Jews were no longer a religion; people who could be converted. They were transformed into a race. A race that had to be exterminated.

On Jan 30,1937, hitler declared, "There is one error which cannot be remedied once men have made it...the failure to recognize the importance of conserving the blood and the race free from intermixture and thereby the racial aspect and character which are God's gift and God's handiwork. It is not for men to discuss the question of why Providence created different races, but rather to recognize the fact that it punishes those who disregard its work of creation. As I look back...my first feeling is one of thankfulness to our Almighty God for having allowed me to bring this work to success." hitler would decide who was a German and "the Jew was no German."

The leitmotif of socialism and the National Socialist state would be to consider and appraise everything under the aspect of race.

hitler wrote in Mein Kampf, "Blood sin and desecration of the race are the original sin in this world and the end of humanity which surrenders to it."

So much energy was expended by Germans on the Jews. Defining them. Defiling them. Demeaning them. Denigrating them. Destroying them.

Imagine the dissemination of this hatred and the increased attacks on Jews all over the world, no matter how small their numbers in their adopted cities and towns, had social media existed during the time of hitler and his Nazi ideology.

And so hitler eagerly took in his hand the gift of the red thread offered by the red serpent.

4

THE CULTURE WAS RIPE FOR TAKEOVER

The great command for Germany to take the lead was not given by any earthly superior. It was given by god, who created our people.

~ adolf hitler

There was in the German people a hunger for connection to something greater, something beyond the poverty, and their sense of helplessness after the resounding and humiliating defeat of World War I. They yearned to return to a time of innocence, to their stories of the Volk that had engendered in them a sense of strength and importance as a unique culture. There was strength in the memories of a time that perhaps had never taken place, but had become romanticized and mythologized.

In the 19th century, organizations developed to raise nationalist consciousness with cultural celebrations like midsummer and yuletide solstice festivals rooted in Norse history. There were study groups to develop appreciation for German history and literature. There was a turning to social, cultural, and political ideals like racism, magic, and a negating of the modern world. The Prussian Kaiser Wilhelm II (1859–1941), Otto von Bismarck (1815–1898), Helmuth Johann Ludwig von Moltke (1848–1916), and Richard Wagner were celebrated and elevated. There was an awakening to the possibility of returning to a golden age with the reunification of Austria and Germany into a theocratic, pan-German realm where non-Germans would have no role.

Above all was the Swastika, a beautiful ancient Indian symbol of "well-being" and "good luck," a runic symbol of the Sun which was obscenely repurposed to become the official Nazi insignia of "racial purity" and a symbol of victory.

From the 19th century, the German people, including the upper and middle classes, were enraptured with a vision of a pan-German empire that divided the world in two—the Teutonic descendants (blonde, blue-eyed, noble, honest, courageous, superior), Aryans, the superior pure race, against the mixed, inferior races, the most inferior of them all being the Jews. With every breath the German citizens inhaled antisemitism. It came packaged in Theosophy and Ariosophy, a system of pseudo-science and mythology disguised as religious history, pioneered by Austrian Guido von List. The Volkisch ideology was conflated with theology, secret societies and practices, imbuing it with religious undertones. As with all fundamentalists, their ideology had its mantra: there is a proper place for everyone and the place of the racially pure Aryan is at the top.

The red thread of antisemitism was picked up by the Ariosophists including Goerg von Schonerer, Arthur de Gobineau (1816–1882), Eugene Karl Duhring, Johann Gotlieb Fichte, Lanz von Liebenfels, and Karl Lueger (1844–1910), the antisemitic mayor of Vienna, and was woven through ideas and symbols from the idealized past and brought forward into the 20th century.

The greatest weaver of all turned out to be Guido von List who started his writing career in 1871 and over time combined Volkisch beliefs, occultism and theosophy, medieval German apocalyptic Norse legends with messianic salvation. He saw the 20th century, the new millennium as the German millennium, with a God-sent German patriarch at the helm to fulfill the religious and political expectations of the oppressed. List invoked the sixteenth century philosopher, Giordano Bruno "O Jove, let the Germans realise their own strength…and they will not be men, but gods." And he turned to a verse in the Norse legend "Voluspa" to tell the people of a benevolent messiah whose time was coming;

A wealthy man joins the circle of counsellors,
A Strong One from Above ends the faction,
He settles everything with fair decisions,
Whatever he ordains shall endure forever.

List described the Strong One from Above as a divine dictator whose sense of order would save the German people from the chaos of the uncertain nature of the modernizing industrial world. At the end of World War I, List offered this belief to the people:

"The Austrian and German victims of the slaughter on the battle-fronts will be reincarnated as a collective messianic body. The hundred thousands of war-dead will be reborn with innate millennial fervour; these young men will form the elite messianic corps in a later post-war national revolution. The year 1932 is the time when a divine force will possess the collective unconsciousness of the German people. This generation of resurrected revolutionaries will become sensitive to the divine force and constitute a fanatic league which will usher in the new age. Order, national revenge, and fervour will then transform this modern pluralist society into a monolithic, eternal, and incorruptible state. This is the blueprint for the future Greater Germanic Reich."

The culture was ripe for takeover. As it had been revealed:

For then I saw an angel come down from heaven with the key to the Abyss in his hand and an enormous chain. He overpowered the dragon that primeval serpent which is the devil and chained him for one thousand years. He hurled him into the Abyss and shut the entrance and sealed it over him, to make sure that he would not lead the nations astray again until the thousand years had passed. At the end of that time he must be released but only for a short while. When the thousand years are over, the devil, Satan, will be released from his prison and will come out to lead astray the nations.

And he did. The serpent slithered forward and reveled in the Third Reich. And in 1933 he revealed himself in adolf hitler, a man of medium height with beady eyes and a comic moustache.

hitler was to become the Nordic Borealis, the light of civilization, blotting out the inferior races. As he said: "I fight to safeguard the existence and reproduction of our race and our people, the sustenance of our children and the purity of our blood, the freedom and independence of the fatherland so that our people

15

may mature for the fulfillment of the mission allotted it by the creator of the universe."

And with the mantle of a superman, this German superhero with a low receding forehead, ugly nose, broad cheekbones, small eyes and dark hair was blessed by his electorate as he swept across Germany and back home to Austria where he marched to the trumpets of glory.

hitler declared: "Just as the Jew could incite the mob of Jerusalem against Christ, so today he must succeed in inciting folk who have been duped into madness to attack those who, God's truth, seek to deal with this people in utter honesty and sincerity."

He spoke to their nostalgia for a past that never was. And they adored him. There they were; tens of thousands of people, including thousands of young people dressed in their Brownshirts; all standing tall waiting for their leader, all screaming,

"We want our Führer! We want our Führer!"

There, at the Nuremberg parade ground; in the Zeppelin Field, bathed in the cathedral of light from one hundred and thirty spotlights, giving the eerie impression that all were surrounded by Grecian-like stone pillars.

Now, close your eyes. Listen. Can you hear it? Can you hear the clicking of hundreds of thousands of pairs of heels in harmony? Listen. Can you hear the beating of the drums? The shattering of glass? Now, the applause. Now, the roar of adulation. Now, the adoration. "Heil hitler, Heil hitler, Heil hitler." Louder, louder, louder. Now, open your eyes. Can you see the red, white and black flags, signifying blood and soil of the Third Reich, cascading down the sides of the ornate buildings; huge, oversized flags, hundreds of them that seem to merge into one huge image of the power of the Reich. And in the middle of it all, at the top of the building, to be seen by all there were the gold-plated Reich's Eagle Hoheitszeichen; the proud eagle, head raised, wings spread, claws wrapped around a wreath of oak leaves cradling the ubiquitous Swastika.

See the thousands upon thousands of hands raised in the Nazi salute. The pomp and circumstance. The pageantry rolled in mystery and mysticism. Wave upon wave of everyday people, dressed in their Sunday finery, lining the grand road, memories of Wotan washing over them, memories of past glories passing before their eyes, weeping with joy, saluting and throwing flowers at their leader as he strides past them, flanked on either side by gigantic formations of Nazis in perfectly aligned columns; as if his authority has been given by god, who created his people.

"Heil hitler Heil hitler, Heil hitler," they cry.

5

THE WINDS OF WOTAN

*For the fascination of evil throws good things into the shade
and the whirlwind of desire corrupts.*

~ Wisdom 4:12

And so the whirling dervish winds of insanity blasted through Europe unleashing Wotan from his crypt, freeing him to dance maniacally across the land like a tornado, wantonly and Capriciously sucking out all the goodness, the mercy and compassion, loving kindness and charity and leaving behind in his wake the monstrous sacrifice of blood and ashes.

There stood the one-eyed and grave-looking bearded old man Wotan, the god of war and wisdom. Spear in hand and accompanied by his two dogs and two ravens he was the supreme Teutonic god and the father of Thor, the god of thunder. It is said that Wotan stabbed himself with his magical spear and then hanged for nine days on the immense world tree, Yggdrasi, so much was his desire to gain infinite knowledge. He gave away one of his eyes just to drink from the magical well of Mimir: the god of knowledge, wisdom and prophecy.

Wotan, the mythic ruler of Valhalla; the father of nine Valkyries and the Walsungs, the father of a race of heroes, had swept across Europe in the 7th and 8th centuries long before Christianity settled across the land, only to fade away. And then that ancient god of storm and frenzy, the unleasher of passions, filled with a lust for battle, the long quiescent Wotan, awoke, like a primordial volcano, to new activity, in a civilized country that had long been supposed to have outgrown the Middle Ages. The German youth embraced Wotan the restless wanderer, creating unrest and stirring up strife. And the great Wotan watched as they shed the blood of sheep in honour of his resurrection.

The faithful votaries of the roving god wandered restlessly along the roads. They raised their arms to the heavens. A roaring wind tore the gates asunder, shrieking and keening, it cast a black coffin before the crowds. It was Wotan who burst open the gates of the fortress of death. And the German people and the peoples of Eastern Europe lived as if possessed, and they set in motion a horror never before seen; a spasmodic unharnessing of all the wings of the soul that rolled it on its course towards perdition.

Did hitler see himself as the new Christ, the messiah to the new chosen people as the leader reincarnated from Teutonic warrior heroes? Perhaps he thought of himself as the Aryan Christ, made in the image of Wotan blowing through life, ravishing, flooding and extinguishing; like a storm, ungraspable. Did he look at his reflection in the mirror and see himself as the great one, the nameless one, whom all can see but no one saw? Did he know that any man who takes himself for God ends up assassinating men?

hitler declared, "The strength the Almighty has given us to use; that in it and through it we may wage the battle of our life...The others in the past years have not had the blessing of the Almighty—of Him Who in the last resort, whatever man may do, holds in his hands the final decision. Lord God, let us never hesitate or play the coward, let us never forget the duty which we have upon us...We are all proud that through God's powerful aid we have become once more true Germans. And now two worlds face one another—the men of God and the men of Satan. The Jew is the anti-man, the creature of another god. He must have come from another root of the human race. I set the Aryan and the Jew over and against each other."

Had not his hero, the great composer Richard Wagner, said that Jews were a destructive influence on the morality of the German nation and that their subversive power stood in stark contrast to the German psyche?

Race had become a new science in the late 1800s. It was said that history proved that Semites didn't possess the harmony of psychical forces that distinguish the Aryans. Rather they are selfish and elusive. And then the German philologists, ethnologists, and philosophers determined that social degeneration was caused by racial degeneration. Arthur de Gobineau wrote, "The racial question overshadows all other problems of history, that it holds the key to them all, and that the inequality of the races from whose fusion people is formed is enough to explain the whole course of its destiny."

By the time hitler put the plans for the Final Solution into place Germany had already developed methods for mass murder.

The idea of an anti-man, and the ease with which one could annihilate them had already been tested in 1904 in the Battle of Hamakari near the Waterberg Plateau where the Herero people were massacred by the Germans. Men. Women. Children. Mowed down. The fleeing survivors escaped into the desert but were kept from the water wells, to die of thirst. Cleansing patrols were established to hunt down any of the Herero and destroy them. Those not murdered, mostly women and children, were put into concentration camps, which were intended to be death camps. Death came from exposure to the elements, working in ice-cold water, constant whipping and indiscriminate shootings. By the time the German army was finished with the Herero only 15,000 of 80,000 remained. The Germans had taken their land and the survivors were turned into slave labourers.

But the Germans were not done. Dr. Eugen Fischer was interested in the new field of race hygiene. Autopsies were done on the Herero for racial-biological research. Skulls, scraped clean by Herero slave labour were sent to Germany for further research. Dr. Fischer published a paper on race in 1913.

"We know this absolutely for sure: without exception, any European people...that has absorbed the blood of less valuable races—and only a zealot can deny that blacks, Hottentots and many others are less valuable(than whites)—has paid for this absorption with its spiritual and cultural downfalls."

Catholics protested against this attitude and against the laws against miscegenation that were established in German South-

West Africa. Yet, these ideas prevailed in Germany and moved forward with even greater evil to follow.

Dr. Fischer went on to write *Human Heredity and Race Hygiene* which he co-authored with Erwin Bauer and Fritz Lens. Published in 1921, the paper became a leader in the field of eugenics and was read by the young adolf hitler while he was in jail for the failed Munich coup of 1923. Fischer's work spoke to him for hitler feared any attempt to dilute the Aryan race. Fischer's work included forced sterilization of children, known as the Rhineland Bastards, parented by Senegalese soldiers stationed in the Rhineland and German women.

One of the students of Eugen Fischer was Josef Mengele. And the serpent wove the red thread around him.

Many of the people in positions of power in hitler's forces were familiar with the massacre of the South-West Africans, the use of slave labour, concentration camps, the cleansing of a portion of land to make room for the German people to grow. There was a desire to replicate in the Eastern Reich that which was accomplished in Africa. Himmler said it succinctly; all Mongrel types had to be replaced with Aryans to create a new blond province.

6

WHO IS LIKE THE BEAST?

The sacrifice of the upright is acceptable, its memorial will not be forgotten.

~ Ecclesiasticus 35:6

hitler, the latest rendition of the Teutonic god spoke to his sycophants.

"The Aryans, by their nature, their blood, were chosen to rule the world. The Aryan race is the bearer of human cultural development and therefore human culture and civilization are inseparably bound up in the presence of the Aryan. What we must fight for is to safeguard the existence and reproduction of our race and our people, the sustenance of our children and the purity of our blood, the freedom and independence of the fatherland, so that our people may mature for the fulfillment of the mission allotted it by the creator of the universe.

"The Jew is the greatest obstacle to the fulfillment of this racial millennium. The mightiest counterpart to the Aryan is represented by the Jew. Whoever knows the Jew knows the devil. The vileness of the Jew is so gigantic that no one need be surprised if among our people the personification of the Devil as the symbol of all evil assumes the living shape of the Jews.

"The vileness of the Jew resides in the blood of the race. If the Jews were alone in this world, they would stifle in filth and offal. They are at the centre of every abscess, germ carriers poisoning the blood of others but preserving their own. Was there any form of filth or profligacy, particularly in cultural life, without at least one Jew involved in it? The poison of the press controlled by the Jews penetrates the bloodstream of our people. The spider is slowly sucking the blood out of the people's pores. It is the inexorable Jew who struggles for his domination over the nations.

"Hence today I believe that I am acting in accordance with the will of the Almighty Creator; by defending myself against the Jew, I am fighting for the work of the Lord. The resurrection of Germany will never be achieved without the clearest knowledge of the racial problem and hence the Jewish problem. And once we finish the Jews of Europe our sole objective will be the destruction of the Jewish element residing in the Arab sphere."

The sickly-sweet smell of death was snaking its way through the air, again. Fear was undulating through the land, beating its drum: waiting, waiting. And from the World to Come, the hidden world, *Olam Haba*, Abraham, Sarah and Isaac stirred. Jesus and Paul cannot believe what they have heard.

Abraham, folding in on himself, holding close to his beloved Sarah and his son Isaac cries, "We see hitler as a reproof to our way of thinking. The very sight of him weighs our spirits down; for his kind of life is not like other people's and his ways are quite different."

Abraham beseeches his God: "Let the upright stand up boldly to face those who oppressed us and thought so little of our sufferings. And seeing us they will be seized with terrible fear. Lord God, King, my God, spare your people! For our ruin is being plotted, there are plans to destroy your ancient heritage. Do not overlook your inheritance, which you redeemed from Egypt to be yours. Hear my supplication, have mercy on your heritage, and turn our grief into rejoicing, so that we may live, Lord, to hymn your name. Do not suffer the mouths of those who praise you to perish."

hitler "Have I not been appointed by God? Is it not demanded, then by God, that all of the people obey me?"

Paul "Everyone is to obey the governing authorities, because there is no authority except from God and so whatever authorities exist have been appointed by God. So anyone who disobeys an authority is rebelling against God's ordinance. Are not all powers that exist ordained by God for your good?"

hitler "Am I not a follower of the teachings of the Church?"

The Church itself separated the Jews from the true believers. The Church prohibited marriage between Jews and Christians and the sharing of meals in the early third century. They denied Jews the right to hold public office. By the sixth century Jews were not allowed to employ Christian servants nor were they allowed to be on the streets during Passion Week. And the snake slithered forward to the 12th Synod of Toledo which declared the burning of Jewish books acceptable. By the end of the 7th century Christians were told not to access medical care from Jewish doctors. In the 11th century Christians were forbidden from living in Jewish homes. In 1078 The Synod of Gerona made it an obligation for Jews to pay taxes to support the Church to the same extent as the Christians. The Third Lateral Council forbad Jews from being witnesses or plaintiffs against Christians.

The red thread had no problem finding a home.

In 1215 the Fourth Lateran Council decreed that Jews must mark their clothing to publicly designate their religion. In 1222 the Council of Oxford prohibited the construction of new synagogues and in 1267 the Synod of Vienna prohibited Christians from attending Jewish ceremonies. In 1267 the Synod of Breslau made Jewish ghettos compulsory. A Christian converting to Judaism was decreed heresy in by the Synod of Mainz in 1310 and in 1434 the Council of Basel denied Jews the ability to obtain academic degrees.

"We are only following in the Path laid down before us."

And so the rant continued. The sordid history of Christianity; the justification for the destruction of the Jewish people. Do not all tyrants justify the irrational, the illogical, the specious, the unthinkable? hitler had history as his defense.

In 1516, the Jews of Venice were pushed into a community, a ghetto, surrounded by water with only one bridge connecting the ghetto to the rest of Venice. The bridge was guarded by a Christian watchman to ensure that no one left during the night. The Jews could leave the Ghetto only after the morning tolling of the bell and only when wearing a yellow tunic and hat. A mark of Cain.

Taken from another time and place when Muslims forced Jews to wear the cloth of the demeaned, the degraded, the dhimmi. In 1555, Pope Paul IV, ordered the Jews of Rome into a ghetto and decreed that they, too, be marked by wearing a yellow star, to separate them from the others. How did the red thread reach so high?

hitler was only following up with more modern ways of stamping "Jew" on the forehead, his rendition of the Scarlet Letter. "A Volkish state must begin by raising marriage from the level of continuous defilement of the race, and give it consecration of an institution which is called upon to produce images of the Lord and not monstrosities half-way between man and ape.

"Thou shalt keep thy blood pure. Consider it a crime to soil the noble Aryan breed of thy people by mingling it with the Jewish breed. For thou must know that Jewish blood is everlasting, putting the Jewish stamp on the body and soul of the farthest generations.

"Thou shalt have no social intercourse with the Jew. Avoid all contact and community with the Jew and keep him away from thyself and thy family, especially thy daughters, lest they suffer injury of body and soul.

"Only those who are our fellow Germans, the great *Volksgenosse*, shall be citizens of our state. Only those who are of German blood can be considered as our fellow Germans regardless of creed. Hence, no Jew can be regarded as a fellow German.

"Germany must once again be captain of her soul and master of her destinies, together with all those who want to join Germany. For our nation to recover its health, the Jewish spirit must be eradicated. Don't be misled into thinking you can fight a disease without killing the carrier, without destroying the bacillus. Don't think you can fight racial tuberculosis without taking care to rid the nation of the carrier of that racial tuberculosis. This Jewish contamination will not subside, this poisoning of the nation will not end, until the carrier himself, the Jew, has been banished from our midst."

As hitler pointed out to his people, "Rational antisemitism, however, must lead to a systematic legal opposition and elimination of the special privileges which Jews hold, in contrast to other aliens living among us. Jews will not hold public office. Jews cannot vote. Jews can no longer practice law or teach. They cannot be jurors or commercial judges. Jews may not own rural property. Jews cannot hold positions in art, literature, theatre, motion pictures. The Jews will be excluded from public life, government, culture and the professions."

And with the enactment of the Nuremberg Laws 1935, anti-Jewish laws were adopted and antisemitism based on race was legalized while turning the purity of German blood into a legal category. More than four hundred laws and decrees were enacted. And the serpent, red thread in hand, slithered forward.

A bureaucracy was established to enforce all these laws and decrees. It was necessary to find all the Jews, learn their occupations, so that they could then be denied the opportunity to work. Laws defining a Jew were enacted. And then each civil servant had to prove their "Aryanism." Questionnaires were developed to ascertain genealogy. And if there were concerns, an opinion needed to be obtained from the expert on racial research attached to the Reich Minister of the Interior. No one with Jewish blood would find work, shelter, safety, peace in this new world order.

hitler: "If at the beginning of the War and during the War, twelve or fifteen thousand of these Hebrew corrupters of the people had been held under poison gas, as happened to thousands of our best German workers in the field, the sacrifice of millions at the front would not have been in vain. I am only following in the footsteps of those who walked this path before me.

"Even Martin Luther realized the error of his ways and condemned the Jews as well. Did he not say that their synagogues should be set on fire; their homes should be likewise broken and destroyed; they should be deprived of their prayer books and Talmuds; their rabbis must be forbidden on pain of death to preach anymore; passports and traveling privileges should be absolutely forbidden to the Jews; they ought to be stopped from usury; let the young and strong Jews and Jewesses be given flail, the ax, the hoe, the spade, the distaff, and spindle and get them to earn their bread by the sweat of their noses."

hitler was well aware of the feelings of Luther toward the Jews from Luther's own words. Had Luther not declared, "In short the Jews are worse than devils. O God, my beloved Father and Creator, have pity on me who, in self-defense, must speak so scandalously of thy divine and eternal Majesty, against thy wicked enemies, the devils and the Jews. You know that I do so in the ardor of my faith and in Thy Majesty's honor, for in my case, the question is one that involves all my heart and all my life. So I declare the final objective must unswervingly be the removal of the Jews altogether."

Taking comfort in the words of Luther, another Amalek, and the previous actions of the Catholics, hitler had no problem declaring: "We are determined as leaders of the nation, to fulfill as a national government the task which has been given to us, swearing fidelity only to God, our conscience, and our Volk. The national government will regard its first and foremost duty to restore the unity of spirit and purpose of our Volk. It will preserve and defend the foundations upon which the power of our nation rests. It will take Christianity, as the basis of our collective morality, and the family as the nucleus of our Volk and state, under firm protection...May God Almighty take our work into his grace, give true form to our will, bless our insight, and endow us with the trust of our Volk. We see our way clearly on the point that the war can end only in that either the Aryan peoples are annihilated or Jewry will disappear from Europe.

"I believe that I am acting in accordance with the will of the Almighty Creator by defending myself against the Jew. I am fighting for the work of the Lord. We are God's people."

And so this 20th century Amalek, the red thread in his grasp, made the annihilation of the Jews go hand in hand with the war.

The people chose to listen to this man, their saviour. They worshipped this beast and gave themselves to him: "Let me tell you quite frankly: in one way or another we will have to finish with the Jews." The führer once expressed it as follows: "Should Jewry once again succeed in inciting a world war, the bloodletting could not be limited to the peoples they drove to war but the Jews, themselves, would be done for in Europe."

Who is like the beast; who can fight against it?

Jesus looks to Paul and says: "He claims to have knowledge of God, and calls himself a child of the Lord. How is this possible? How did this come to be? Everywhere a welter of blood and murder, theft and fraud, corruption, treachery, riot, perjury, disturbance of decent people, forgetfulness of favours, pollution of souls, sins against nature. For the worship of idols with no name is the beginning, cause, and end of every evil. For these people either carry their merrymaking to the point of frenzy, or they prophesy what is not true, or they live wicked lives, or they perjure themselves without hesitation; since they put their trust into false idols they do not reckon their false oaths can harm them."

7

A Fire Offering

And the priest shall cause it to go up in smoke on the altar, consumed as a fire offering, [with] a pleasing fragrance. All sacrificial fat belongs to the Lord.

~ Leviticus 3:16

Jesus; "Is the priest burning a sacrifice on the altar as a burnt offering to God? There are flames to the very sky, a sky darkened by a cloud."

Abraham: "This must be the glory of God, filling the dwelling."

"Can it be true," asks Sarah "that we will find God here?"

"It must be," replied Abraham, "Does not the cloud of God stay over our people until it is time to move on? And look there is fire inside the cloud for the House of Israel to see. Is God once again showing His glory and His greatness, will we hear His voice from the heart of the fire? Is this a new Temple for the indwelling of our Lord?"

The Temple in Jerusalem with its forty-five foot coffered ceiling had reached up into the blue velvet sky over the sacred city of Jerusalem. It was an extraordinary piece of architecture, an elegant and awesome home, to hold the place of glory for the Lord. It had taken King Solomon, son of David, seven years to complete on Mount Moriah, the place of the Akedah, the binding of Isaac, where Abraham had brought his only son to sacrifice to God. The grounds of the Temple Mount were built like a rectangular layer cake, each layer narrower than the one below. The entrance to the lowest storey of the temple, the Court of the Women was at the right hand quarter with a spiral staircase leading to the middle story of the compound, The Court of the Israelites for male Jews and then from there to the top, nearest the central building, bordered by two huge bronze pillars known as Boaz and Jachin, was the Court of

Priests, where the Priests conducted the sacrifices and the services.

The Temple had been built of cedar and cypress wood from Tyre with quarry dressed stone on top of huge foundational stones. The cedar within the house was covered in glorious carved figures of winged creatures, palm trees and rosettes, and the Temple walls were laced with windows, wide on the outside and narrow on the inside so that Wisdom could beam its light throughout the world. And the floors, they, too, were overlaid in gold.

And Solomon, who built the Temple for the name of God, made a place for the ark containing the covenant between God and his ancestors when He brought them out of Egypt, out of slavery to freedom. The Sanctuary, holding the Holy of Holies, was made of walls glittering in gold and had two winged creatures, cherubim, made of olive-wood covered in gold facing each other, with their wings spread upwards, protecting the Ark of the Covenant, the one carried through the wilderness containing the tablets of law. And Solomon made doors of olive-wood for the entrance to the Sanctuary and carved figures of cherubim and palm trees and open flowers and overlaid them with gold. There were pillars of brass topped with brass capitals covered in wreaths of chain-work. There were carvings of pomegranates, the symbol of righteousness; because it is said that the pomegranate has 613 seeds, the number of mitzvoth, commandments in the Torah. How virtuous were these carvings on the pillars, symbols of knowledge, wisdom and learning.

And Solomon built a pool for water on top of twelve carved oxen facing outward, three in each direction. And all the utensils, and the table for the loaves of permanent offering, the candlesticks the lamps, tongs, basins and snuffers, the sprinkling bowls, the incense ladles and the fire pans, and the door panels for the inner shrine, and the hinges, were all overlaid in gold. Inside and out, the Sanctuary, the whole house was overlaid in gold as if trying to reflect the Glory of God. And the cloud, the glory of God, who walked with His people through the desert, filled the Temple.

And the Temple grounds were a gathering place, like a market. It was the centre of the Jewish community and the one place that the Jewish people from all around the countryside would come to honour God. Merchants and priests. So many people bringing offerings to God, for gratitude, for penance, for peace. Animals everywhere; doves, bulls, oxen, sheep and goats, for the offerings to God.

Sacrifices were offered everyday by the priests. The greatest celebrations and offerings took place three times a year during the Pilgrim in-gatherings, the festivals; The Tabernacles in the fall, Passover in the spring and Pentecost in the summer. The holiest of days took place in the fall on Yom Kippur, the Day of Atonement, the only time in the year when the priest entered the Holy of Holies to pray for the forgiveness of the people. The priest would be adorned in his special garments; a tunic with a sash, over which was placed a robe. The ephod, gold and embroidered was then placed over the robe. The breastplate containing twelve stones representing the twelve tribes of Israel was overlaid on the ephod. And upon his head rested the turban with a golden head plate, held in place by three threads tied at the back of the head.

There were rules regarding the sacrifices. If his offering is to be an animal from the flock, a lamb or a goat to be offered as a burnt offering, he must be of an unblemished male. The priest slaughters it on the north side of the altar, pours blood all around, and then burns it all on the altar as a burnt sacrifice, an offering made by fire, of a sweet savour unto the Lord. The fire on the altar that consumes the burnt offering must not be allowed to go out. Each morning the priest will make it up with wood, arranging the burnt offering on it and burning the fat from the communion sacrifices. The fire must always be burning. This is the ritual for the burnt offering that stays on the altar brazier all night until morning and is consumed by the altar fire.

31

And so Abraham, Sarah, Isaac, Jesus and Paul make their way toward the cloud hovering overhead, just beyond the fence. But the scent from the sacrifice was not as remembered. Jesus remembered going up to Jerusalem into the Temple where he had found people selling cattle and sheep and doves and the money changers sitting there. Making a whip out of a cord, he had driven them all out of the Temple, sheep and cattle as well as scattering the money-changers coins. He had knocked their tables over and had said to the dove sellers "Take all this out of here and stop using my Father's house as a market."

It wasn't that Jesus was against the sacrifices. It was more that he feared that his people had forgotten the meaning of the sacrifices, the rituals meant to remind the people of their obligations to their God; the God of Abraham, the God of Isaac and the God of Jacob.

"Do not imagine that I have come to abolish the Law or the Prophets. I have come not to abolish but to complete them. In truth I tell you, till heaven and earth disappear, not one jot not one tittle, is to disappear from the Law until all its purpose is achieved."

This scent in the air was different.

Isaac stood back, hesitating. He looked at the cloud and remembered. He still harboured memories of that day on Mount Moriah, the three days walking and climbing, carrying the wood on his back on the last part of the journey. He remembered wondering, where is the sacrifice? And he helped to build the altar. And then he had frozen with the knowledge that he was to be the sacrifice. All those memories flooded back, almost paralysing him, again. He remembered the love he had for his mother and the fear that he would never see her again, or tell her how much he adored her. He had worried about her. What would his father Abraham have said to her? How would she have ever understood?

8

ELIE'S JOURNEY

And tomorrow you'll be wiggling skyward as smoke from this chimney.

~ The Final Solution, the answer to the
Jewish Question

Elie, a young boy on the cusp of adulthood had just celebrated his Bar Mitzva. He had stood in front of his people, read from the Holy Scripture, led the congregation in prayer and rejoiced with them in a common meal prepared by the women of his village. It was a glorious day. He was now an adult in the eyes of his community. He had new obligations, responsibilities and duties. You could see in his face, the young man he would become. Some would say that he was a beautiful boy. He had a full head of tight curly black hair, with short side curls and thick dark eyebrows over eyes that were so brown they appeared black in certain light. His lashes were so long when he lowered his gaze they brushed his cheeks. He had a straight proud nose above full lips. His cheeks gave him away. They still had the look of baby fat. You could see that he would be tall and broad. He thought of himself as an observant Jew, constantly studying the Torah and Talmud, weeping over the loss of the Temple, God's place.

Some would say that he was bewitched by the holy books. He would caress the books, softly, feel the pages and hear the word of his God through the blaring of the trumpets and the soft sounds of the strings of the harp. The voice he heard was not in the great and mighty wind, splitting the mountains and shattering the rocks by the power of God. Nor was the voice in the earthquake that came after the wind. Nor was it in the fire that came after the earthquake. But the voice of God was in the sound of delicate silence that came after the fire.

33

He had learned at a young age the power of questions. "Man raises himself toward God by the questions he asks." It is in the questioning, why is this night different from all other nights, that we reach up and out of ourselves in search of the unknown. His teacher had told him to pray that God would give him the strength to ask Him the right question. What were the right questions to ask in Hungary in 1944?

For a thirteen year old, he was well beyond his years. Perhaps he had been born with an old soul. He wanted to know the secrets of Jewish mysticism. He yearned for knowledge of the divine essence. Instead, he discovered the meaning of ghetto, of unparalleled hate. Two years later, the Nazi horror show failing and the Russians at the front, the Nazis continued their quest to rid the world of the Jews. Despite the shortage of railcars, cars needed for war transport, they continued to transport millions of Jews to the east into their enormous, costly extermination factories. Elie found himself along with his father, mother and two sisters boarding one of those trains.

In the spring of 1944, a time of hope and renewal, when the trees were covered in a riot of colourful blooms, the families of his little village were put into a rolling convoy of cattle cars. They were being sent into exile, *galut*. But this one would be different. Unlike those before who had been taken away to Babylonia, they were never to return to the land of their people, for they will be turned into dust to be blown away in the wind.

They were eighty people to a car; human beings filled with dreams and hopes and promise. Pious Jews, wrapped in their prayer shawls, marched into the trains, prepared for martyrdom, for the glorification and sanctification of God, convinced that their sacrifice was required as testimony to Almighty God. Their provisions included a few loaves of bread and some water. No room to lie down. The quiet claustrophobia was broken by curses and kicks. There was very little air. No toilets. After two days of travel all were tortured by thirst. The heat became unbearable. The stench, insufferable. But everything that breathes will praise God. The breath of all that live will bless Your name.

While Jews were being transported in one direction to their death, happy passengers, dressed in their Sunday finest, sitting in well-appointed trains, rolled by in the other direction. They had no choice but to close their windows tightly to avoid the foul smell that drifted over them from the death trains. Can you imagine their discomfort? Paying for a ticket to go from here to there, to family, to business. Enjoying the scent of spring, looking forward to their Easter celebrations; the Passion of Christ. And interrupted by the scent of decay and death. It is difficult to say which of the sounds was louder; the forlorn wailing sound of the whistle of the passenger train as it roared by or the mournful keening of all of in the train to hell?

And there was Sarah, the rose of Sharon, a lily among the thorns, here to witness. Our Mother, Sarah, walking through the boxcars, holding the hands of the little ones, caressing the faces of the elderly, watching helplessly as the mothers, nursing their young ones, begged for water.

Her weeping so great, her grief so insurmountable that words could never express, she once again turned the pain inward as she had when she heard about Isaac on Mount Moriah. Her agony was shrieked in silence.

Opening her soul to the Shekhina, the Holy Spirit she cried, "Every hour I suffer agonies of heart, while I strive to understand the way of the Most High...For it would have been better for the dust not to have been born, so that the mind might not have been made from it...and we are tormented."

Had not Metatron, the archangel Michael, sacrificed the souls of the saints in order to atone for the sins of Israel in the days of their exile? What more was wanted?

She wept as her children withered, and held her hands to her ears as others went mad, screaming at visions only they could see. But nothing that they imagined could ever be as evil as what turned out to be true.

And Elie carried on. "At last there was relief from the cars. We had arrived. Standing in the rail cars for days at a time, legs weakened, buckling beneath. We almost fell out of the cars we were so tightly packed. Many were already dead. Yet the air for which I had yearned for so many days, to take a breath, the air was filled with the smell of burning flesh. Then I saw the flames gushing out of a tall chimney as if it were breathing out fire while puffing out stinking smoke into the black sky. There it was; a pillar of blazing fire, a guide to my unknown journey."

And Sarah witnessed boxcar after boxcar of death waiting to exhale. "Look there, a boy. Like my Isaac. So innocent. And there, like Jacob and Rachel and Benjamin and Judah, Tamar, Yael and Deborah. They are all here, huddled together. You took them out of Egypt. You watched over them by night in a pillar of fire and by day in a pillar of smoke and yet now when they, when we, when I need You, my children, Your children, they are not being led by a pillar of smoke into freedom but marched into the ovens to be turned into pillars of smoke."

Elie continued: "I stood for selection, watching others sent to their deaths. I had wasted away on rations that would not feed a field mouse. Emaciated, I followed rules, new ones and old ones, always changing, never making sense. *Schnell, schnell ,schnell.* Move, move, move. Faster, faster, faster.

"I watched as the women and girls undressed and had their hair completely cut off. They transformed before my eyes from people to things. They were marched in files between auxiliary police, hurried along with whips, sticks or guns, to wait naked in front of the doors adorned with beds of blood red flowers. I listened to the SS guard tell them that no harm will come to them. Just breathe very deeply, that strengthens the lungs, inhaling is a means of preventing contagious diseases. It is good disinfection. Don't worry. After this the men will have work, building roads and houses. The women will do housekeeping and cooking. Why not believe this little story. How is one to know friend from foe when all around is the surreal?

"And I listened as they whispered their last words: My God, the soul You have placed within me is pure; You created it, fashioned it, and breathed it into me. You constantly safeguard it for me and eventually You will take it from me to be restored only in the hereafter. Yet, as long as it is within me I will gratefully give thanks to You, O Lord, in Whose Hands are the souls of all the living."

Isaac was there; watching. He remembered how he had followed his father's instructions. Carry the wood. Place it on the altar. Then lie down to be sacrificed. He had gone so meekly to the fire pit. Why, he wondered had he not fought? And now he watched as his sisters marched so meekly up a small flight of wooden stairs to become fuel for the gas chamber and the crematoria. One person per square foot. They were gassed for 10–30 minutes. And Sarah was there, too, first to console her daughters, as they waited like sheep to slaughter and then as her girls marched into the circle of hell. Sarah, the love of Abraham's life. Sarah, with thick, black wavy hair shot through with threads of gold, fair as the moon, resplendent as the sun, and eyes like the pools of Heshbon.

Sarah: "These people are not satisfied with the bitterness of our slavery; they have pledged themselves to abolish the decree that you have uttered, to blot out your heritage, your people, chosen to share your teachings of compassion to all. They pledge to stop the mouths of those who praise you, to quench your altar and the glory of your House, and instead to open up the mouths of the heathen and to forever idolize a king of flesh. Never let our ruin be a matter for laughter. Turn these plots against their authors, and make an example of the man who leads the attack on us."

And when at last the room was opened they were like pillars of basalt, still erect, not having any space to fall.

To make room for the next load the bodies were tossed out; blue, wet with sweat and urine, legs covered with feces and menstrual blood into an excavator that carried the bodies to be burned in the open air or crematoria. The Nazis were not ones to be wasteful. Before the Sonderkommando, the special commando of Jewish workers who put the dead into the crematoria, many times their own family members, other workers checked the mouths of the dead, catching them like a fish on a hook, tossing those with gold in their teeth one way and those without, the other.

This was too much for Jesus to bear. "Why did you let them put me on the cross, to be humiliated, to suffer for their sins and yet, here I am walking through the ashes of Your children and My children, for they are mine, too.

"I thought I was the one, the sacrifice for all humanity. I was the one to die for all of their sins. You said it was foretold, by Isaac and Isaiah. Yet, here I am, walking through the ashes of your children, the children of Abraham and Sarah. Look about me. How could this happen? My eyes: They burn with dry, bloody tears, the blood of Your children. So many, so many, unfathomable."

Isaac watched, remembering the death of his mother: how he had gently placed her into the ground; praying over her, that her soul should return to sit at the right side of God under the protection of the wings of the Shekhina. He remembered taking five smooth stones that he had carried with him from the time he was a child and placing them on her grave. Yet, here he witnessed his people, throwing their parents into the crematoria like cordwood on a bonfire. He mourned for the sons, not able to pray over the souls of their parents or mark their graves, or say Kaddish for them to help the soul of the deceased in its journey upwards each year as he had done for his own mother. As the sages of the Talmud say, "A parent can bring a child into this world, but a child can bring a parent into the world to come."

And Isaac remembered Amalek; "Had Saul but listened to God, had he punished Amalek for his attacks against the newly freed Jews leaving Egypt, had he crushed Amalek, put him under the curse of destruction with all that he possessed, perhaps evil would have been removed from the earth."

But for hitler this was all in a day's work: "Gentlemen, if there were ever, after us, a generation so cowardly and so soft that they

38

could not understand our work which is so good, so necessary, then, gentlemen, all of National Socialism will have been in vain. We ought, on the contrary, to bury bronze tablets stating that it was we who had the courage to carry out this gigantic task."

9

MEMORY IS THE SCRIBE OF THE SOUL

The fanatical populace of Western Europe vented its blind rage and its fear-crazed hysteria, which came to be known as the "red laughter" upon the hapless Jews in their midst.

~ J.B. Agus

The pile of the murdered grew. After a few days the bodies swelled and the heap grew by three to six feet as the gut bacteria began to digest the intestines and then the surrounding tissues; from the inside out, feeding on the body tissues, fermenting the sugars. And the bodies expanded from the build-up of methane, hydrogen sulphide and ammonia, which accumulate within the body, first in the abdomen and sometimes other body parts, too. The foul, sickly sweet odour of death hung over the mound and blowflies attracted to the smell of incipient decay engulfed the bloated bodies, laying eggs in the orifices and open wounds.

There was no place to hide from the horror of death. A maniacal red laugh rose from the bowel of mother earth as the people, infected by the violence and madness of war, maimed and murdered and rejoiced in the blood sacrifice of the Jews. The red laugh echoed through the valleys of death. How ironic. For is not the name of the land "*adom*"—red. And was not Adam named for the red land?

Later, the decaying bodies were piled onto train rails and burned in diesel oil. Wiped from memory. There were just too many to burn in the crematoria so they had to be burned in open pits.

hitler told Abraham, Sarah, Isaac, Jesus and Paul: "The work of the Nazis is a great work and a very useful and very necessary duty...When one sees the bodies of the Jews, one understands the greatness of their work."

At the end of a hard day at work the Nazis, Mengele, Hess Karl Hoecher and Enno Lolling and their fellow officers, relaxed with the women who aided and abetted in the mass murder of Jews who now sat on the deck playing with their children. They spent their time at a resort a mere twenty miles away, laughing and dancing and singing, eating and drinking to the raucous sounds of the accordion playing their beloved marching song "Die Fahne Hoch" the Nazi anthem written in 1929 by Sturmfuhrer Horst Wessel, a university educated, son of a pastor, who was the commander of the Nazi paramilitary Brownshirts.

"Clear the streets for the brown battalions,
Clear the streets for the storm division!
Millions are looking upon the swastika, full of hope,
The day of freedom and of bread dawns!
Soon Hitler's banners will flutter above the barricades."

Yet there was time to complain about of all things—a lack of blueberries.

And what of the doctors who relaxed at the resort? Who declared that they wanted to preserve life? And out of respect for human life said they would of course remove a gangrenous appendix from a diseased body. But what of killing a Jew? Not a problem for them. For the Jew, to them was a gangrenous appendix in the body of mankind. So murdering Jewish men women and children in the morning and then cavorting in the evening was no problem, either.

Amazing.

To be able to sort people; "You to the right and life; You to the left and death. Popping the Zyklon B into the showers. Suffocating men women and children, then overseeing the removal of the bodies to the indoor and outdoor crematorium to be turned into ashes blowing in the air. And then going to a resort. To play with their own children; after murdering the children of others.

How was that possible?

Evil. Evil makes it possible.

And it was evil that came from the siren call of Romanticism, a call to return to the inchoate memory of some long ago mythologized innocence of nature that opened the door to the removal of all restraints; freeing people from the repressive mask of civility imposed on them by ethical monotheism, and then, by declaring the death of God it was all too easy to reconnect to the instinctive and intuitive natural man.

And Abraham, the proud patriarch, rich in livestock, silver and gold, respected and loved for his hospitality and friendliness, always welcoming the hungry, offering food and shelter found himself helpless, standing at the side, wondering how the sacrifice of the bull, a burnt offering, on the wood on the fire on the altar, food burnt as a smell pleasing to God at the Tent of Meeting, had become the burnt sacrifice of the Jews. "God, come back, we pray, look down from heaven and see, visit this vine; protect what your hand has planted. They have thrown it into the fire like dung."

So Abraham and Sarah thought of their other children, so many. They remembered how many had died praising the God of Abraham, Isaac and Jacob, with the words of the Shema, the Jewish creed, "Hear O Israel the Lord our God the Lord is One," on their lips; the same prayer beseeched by Jewish martyrs since the time of Rabbi Akiva. They remembered the cry of Rabbi Hananiah ben Teradion wrapped in the Scroll of the Law as he was burned alive. And he called out: "The parchments are being burnt but the letters are soaring on high." Perhaps those letters will carry with them the memories of those who have died with no name, those who perished as if they never lived and those who will return to the Source too early with no one to remember them. Then they remembered those who had been destroyed in the 4th century accused of being killers of the prophets, and murderers of the Lord. Was it not Origen who declared "the Jews...nailed Christ to the cross?"

Abraham, the great ancestor of a host of nations, and Sarah, a woman of valour, recalled the days of the Crusaders. They remembered the murder of their children by the Crusaders on their way from Rouen in Normandy to Jerusalem to liberate the Holy city from the Muslims. Eleven hundred sacrificed in one day in the communities of the Rhine. They remembered Godfrey of Bouillon who reveled in the death of the Jews by fire, shutting them in a synagogue and burning them alive.

Godfrey had learned well from those who had once oppressed the Christians. There was a time when Christians faced great discrimination under Roman rulers. Christians in the early years had been caught in mob violence condemned and burned alive. In 177 in Lyons, Christians had been denied access to public places like the baths and the markets. And then one day, a mob broke loose. Christians were hounded and attacked openly. They were treated as public enemies, assaulted, beaten and stoned. In the first decade of the 4th century CE, Diocletian ordered soldiers to destroy churches, burn religious books, take away civil rights and police protection from those calling themselves Christian. Church leaders were arrested and all efforts made to force them to sacrifice to the Roman gods. Some followers were tortured with hot irons searing their eye sockets. Others were dragged into the Forum where accused of being Christian they confessed and were flung in prison.

And yet, in 1190, the mobs in England, aroused by the mighty Crusades, massacred the Jews of Norwich and those in Stamford and Bury St. Edmunds, Lincoln and Lynn, and then the Jews of London. Abraham and Sarah remembered the spilling of Jewish blood in the pogroms of the 13th century in Frankfurt and Ortenburg, in the state of Bavaria; in Pfortzheim and Speyer; the murders of Jews in Mainz and Cracow, on Passover 1283; the burning of young and old in Munich 1285; the murdered of Trerbach and the murdered of Kemeno near Dusseldorf and the murdered of Bonn.

And there, just beyond their vision, the serpent had lain in waiting; watching.

They mourned for their children who in 1348, accused of causing the Black Plague, were murdered in Mainz and then

Oppenheim, Frankfurt, Erfurt and Cologne, and they mourned those buried in a common grave in Worms. They wept for their Spanish children, living in the seventy communities in Castile and the thirty–six in Aragon, tens of thousands of Jewish people murdered, in 1391 and the extinction of the Jewish community of Majorca and the killing in Barcelona.

They relived the burning of Jews in the 15th century in Breslau and the market-place in Berlin, accused of desecrating the "host," and the murder of the Jews of Trent, accused of killing a Christian boy to use his blood in the making of Matza for Passover. And those burned at the stake, auto da fés, in Spain in the 15th century at the hands of the state, a Catholic state, and the rampages of the 16th century against their children in Rome and throughout Italy, Switzerland and Germany when the Passion plays led to the screaming for Jewish blood.

There was the massacre of Jews by the Cossacks and the Poles in the 17th century led by the Russian tyrants Chmielnicki and Krivonos; children killed at their mothers' breast or roasted alive on spits over the fire. And the pogroms throughout Russia in the 19th and 20th centuries and then, again, the greatest barbarism flowing out of the Nazis.

How many times must they witness seas of flame raging over the fields, burning their children simply because they are Jewish? It was as if Sarah and Abraham were destined to suffer with all their children, over and over again, for some unintended sin for which they had not made proper sacrifice. Was Abraham to be forced to replay in perpetuity to do penance for binding his son and Sarah to cry over the memory of that day?

Memory. Was it not Aristotle who said memory is the scribe of the soul?

10

DANCE ME, LORD, DANCE TO THE END OF LOVE

Mickey Mouse is the most miserable ideal ever revealed...Healthy emotions tell every independent young man and every honourable youth that the dirty and filth-covered vermin, the greatest bacteria in the animal kingdom, cannot be the ideal type of animal...Away with Jewish brutalization of the people. Down with Mickey Mouse! Wear the Swastika!

~ newspaper article, Pomerania Germany,
mid–1930s

Sarah's heart had broken when she heard what had taken place on Mount Moriah. She ached for her son. The fear he must have felt. How helpless he must have been. She cried for her husband. Abraham had been prepared to offer their son, their only son as a burnt offering, an *ola,* an offering to be totally consumed, a holocaust, to God. What must Abraham have been thinking, feeling? Was it fear? Abraham had taken the wood of the burnt offering and laid it on Isaac's back so that his son carried the means of his own death up the mountain. And her son, her only son, was bound on the altar upon the wood. Each time she remembered what might have been she trembled. And it was not long after the binding of Isaac that Sarah came to know God for the first time.

Yet, here she was walking paths paved with the bloated, putrefying bodies of her people; witnessing the death of her children, seeing them rising in the smoke from a great furnace. Sarah thought of all of them as her children. Was not the promise made first to her husband Abraham that he would be exceedingly fruitful and that this covenant would be passed to his children and his children's children for all eternity? Did not this covenant pass to her son, her only son, Isaac? Was not the promise made that Isaac would be blessed with children to equal the stars in heaven and sand which is on the sea shore? And here, here there is an industrialized assembly line designed to create the death of that promise. How could any mother bear such pain?

And so Sarah cried to God. "Do you remember God, when I laughed thinking now that I am past the age of childbearing, and my husband is an old man, is pleasure to come my way again? You asked Abraham, my husband of many years, 'Why did Sarah laugh and say am I really going to have a child now that I am old?' I had watched all the others blossom, fill up and out, walking proudly, knowing that they were fulfilling Your commandment to be fruitful and multiply. I watched; I attended them; I gave Hagar to my beloved to fulfill His obligation. And then You gave to me a son. A perfect son. A beautiful boy to be the first of many, of a nation greater than the grains of sand and more plentiful than the stars in Your heaven. I laughed when I heard you say to Abraham that I would bear fruit. How foolish to promise a withered old woman a child. And then I laughed when I felt life within me. Such joy, such disbelief. And I made all the preparations for my child. And I laughed when my labour began. There would be no pain for me. I know that You had told Eve that we would suffer when giving birth. But not me. How could I suffer, when I, Sarah, an old woman, was bringing my son into the world? And now I know. It was hubris.

"Perhaps if I had not laughed when You said I would be fertile; perhaps if I had not laughed when I felt the quiver of life; perhaps if I had not laughed while bringing this gift into the world; perhaps if I had suffered while labouring; perhaps then the children of my child would be alive. And I think of the tears I shed when I believed that my beloved had taken my child, the fruit of my womb to give to you on Mount Moriah. How shameful of me. How weak and selfish. Perhaps it was my weeping that stayed Your hand. Perhaps You heard me through the mist on Mount Moriah. I rue the day. How could I not? If only You had taken him then I would not be here walking through the valley of death, the killing fields of the Nazis. Remember You told me that nothing is impossible for God? Remember? What of this that we are witnessing? The people moaning to You. Crying out to You. If You can make me fertile when I am so old, why can You not save my children?"

And there was Sarah. Lost. Hopeless. Helpless. Trapped in her own mind. Looking for a way out. And so she sang and danced, twirling and swirling through her memories; oblivious to all but her Maker.

There she was dancing with her King with a burning violin, begging Him to gather her in safely and lift her like an olive branch and be her homeward dove. She was dancing with her Lord, witnessing the horror to the end of love. Lost in her fantasy she was dancing to her wedding now, dancing on and on, dancing, oh so tenderly, to the end of love. She was dancing with the children asking to be born, crying out to Him to raise a tent of shelter now though every thread is torn.

Dance me, Lord, dance to the end of love.

Abraham, father to all, fell to his knees and cried out, "Sovereign Lord, holy and true, how long before You judge and avenge our blood on the inhabitants of earth? You are the Upright One, He who is, He who was, the Holy One. They spilt the blood of the saints and prophets, and blood is what You must give them to drink, is that what they deserve.

"I stand here, helpless, a man who once bravely fought our enemies. I was powerful and feared as You had intended. What is it that You know that we are not meant to see?"

Isaac calls to Jesus: "Does the messiah not cast Israel's oppressors into a fiery pit, raising the righteous back to life, and reign in the New Jerusalem? Why do I hear the voices of my brothers and sisters howling from the depths of the earth?"

Abraham, Sarah, Isaac, and Jesus, witnessing the killing of the infants of the holy ones embraced each other tightly under Abraham's prayer shawl, given to him by God, his Father, worn but not tattered, its long fringes gently frayed from being stroked over and over. He held it gently, lovingly, a canopy floating over them and together they recited the mournful prayer for the dead who will leave no trace in anyone's memory:

"*Yitgadal v'yitkadash sh'may raba*. Exalted and honoured be the name of the Holy One, blessed be He, whose glory transcends, is beyond all blessings and hymns, praises and consolations which are uttered in the world. May there be abundant peace from heaven and life for us all in Israel."

Bending their knees slowly, foreheads toward the ground, they swayed first to the left, and then to the right, then back to the center and prayed:

"May He who established peace in the heavens, grant peace unto us and unto all Israel and let us say Amen," and then they swayed to the left once more.

Abraham raised his voice to Paul. "Look around you. See the incineration of God's children."

And Paul looked around. The sun was black as coarse sackcloth; the moon turned red as blood all over, and the stars of the sky fell onto earth like figs dropping from a fig tree when a high wind shakes it; the sky disappeared like a scroll rolling up and all the mountains and islands were taken from their places.

"I don't understand. How did such evil grip the world?"

Isaac turns to Paul. "Did you not say that submitting to authority—civil authority—you submit to the authority, the government because those in authority have been appointed by God—to disobey authority is rebelling against God? And then did you not preach so long ago 'Your stubborn refusal to repent is only storing up retribution for yourself on that Day of retribution when God's just verdicts will be made known? He will repay everyone as their deeds deserve. Trouble and distress will come to every human being who does evil—the Jews first.' What did you expect?"

Paul responds, "I never intended for this to happen"

Isaac replies "Intentions? From your mouth came a sharp sword that has stricken the children of Israel. Your words have turned into weapons in the hands of those bathed in evil. You taught that guilt is transmitted. This, all of this," he sweeps his hand around the babies burning in the flames, "this is the unintended conse-quences of your words. May God forgive you, pardon you, and grant you atonement."

Jesus looks to Paul. "And if you understood the meaning of my words: Mercy is what pleases me, not sacrifice, you would not have condemned the blameless. Did I not say whatsoever you do to the least of my brothers? These are God's beloved, the most impor-tant people on earth. From the beginning they were the teachers, spreading the word to feed the hungry, to give water to the thirsty, to welcome the stranger, to clothe the naked, to care for the sick, to visit those in prison."

Jesus, Sarah, Abraham and Isaac gather together, once more. "Lord our God, hear our cry, spare them, have mercy and accept our prayer. Give heed to our words. Cast them not away from your presence. Do not take your Holy Spirit away from them. Do not discard them, your Holy people. For they are your people, your children, your servants. They are your community, your posses-sion. They are your flock and you are their Shepherd. They are your creation and you their Creator. They have been your faithful and you their beloved. Do not ignore our pleas."

11

THE END OF THE ROAD

Fools said I, You do not know. Silence like a cancer grows. Hear my words that I might teach you. Take my arms that I might reach you.

~ Paul Simon

The Red Army was closing in on the Nazis from the east and that meant the concentration camps. Would this mean the end of the torture of the Jews? Not in Elie's camp.

The remnant, arms marked by the beast, half-dead, poorly clothed, with sunken faces and rotten teeth marched in freezing cold, blustering snow, under the watchful eyes of their torturers.

"We were not permitted to rest, to slow down; just run, run, run—to where? Soldiers shooting to kill if you stopped. Frozen corpses; one corpse looking like another covered with diaphanous crystal patterned snowflakes. Forty-two miles behind us, how many more to go? To another camp. To more selections. Selections? What was there left to select? Who shall live and who shall die? Who was living? Who was dead? The Red Army was encroaching and the Nazis are stopping to select? Marched, again, into a field, a heavy blanket of snow covering all. A train. We were waiting on a train to take us away, again."

Waiting on one of the hundreds of trains that had been arranged by Eichmann in Budapest March 1944 to carry a half million people to Auschwitz. A new branch line was being built to bring the cars within a few yards of the crematoria. The number of death commandos manning the gas chambers grew from 224 to 860. Not even the war would get in the way of ridding the world of its Jews.

"We were watched over by soldiers so that we not escape. Escape? To where? Ten days and ten nights. No food, no water. No room. Corpses were collected to be removed from the cars, tossed into fields we passed as we made our way through Germany. And then we stopped. We had arrived at Buchenwald."

Soldiers, weapons, manpower and coal for the trains, and dogs, all working to cleanse the land of Jews, while all around the German war effort was failing.

For three more months the Nazis guarded the living-dead. To the end, the Nazis would put their manpower into the service of eliminating all traces of the Jews of Europe. Their primary focus, the order of the day was to come to grips with the Jewish problem. The liquidation of the Jews was the reason for involving Hungary in the war, for keeping her away from the Allies. In the end another million Jews were liquidated—as the Nazis liked to say.

Elie followed the others into the gas chamber. Through his tears Elie could be heard whispering, "My days are over; going up in smoke and my bones will burn like an oven. God, we have heard for ourselves, our ancestors have told us, of the deeds you did in their days, in days of old, by your hand. For Your sake we are being massacred all day long, treated as sheep to be slaughtered? Wake, Lord! Why are You asleep? Awake! Do not abandon us for good. Why do You turn your face away, forgetting that we are poor and harassed? We are bowed down to the dust and lie prone on the ground. Arise! Come to our help! Ransom us, for the sake of the spilt blood of your servants and for the sake of those slain for your holy name. For the sake of the young, blameless school children and for the sake of the infants who have not sinned. For the sake of the bereaved orphans and widows. For your own sake, if not for ours, save us as your faithful love demands.

"Gold is tested in the fire, and the chosen in the furnace. Like the furnace that was made seven times hotter and like Shadrach, Meschak and Abed-Nego before us, we have been thrown into the burning fiery furnace."

Elie lived long enough to see children putting their own dead parents into the crematory oven. Of the 437,000 Jews from

Hungary who were brought to Auschwitz, 352,000 were murdered.

"I looked into the faces of little children, whose bodies were turned into wreaths of black smoke unfurling in the silent sky. The flames leaped out high above the furnace. It looked as if a star had fallen from the sky and opened a shaft in the earth leading down to the Abyss. Smoke rose out of the Abyss like smoke from a huge furnace so that the sun and the sky were darkened by the smoke from the Abyss. It was as if the angels of death had opened their mouths and released smoke and sulphur on the earth and killed a third of the Jewish people."

And for hitler this was ecstasy. It reminded him of the torchlight parades in Nuremburg. He felt as if he had come from heaven right out of the clouds to his adoring people crying out their love for him. Their Aryan Christ.

Isaac, after his binding at Moriah, had devoted his life and his right to immortality through his seed to the defense of his people. And so he marches along the ramp with Elie into the showers in cell number 27 in Block 11 (although all knew it was the gas chamber), touching his siblings, praying, crying and then falling into silence for there are no words for such suffering, no prayers, no understanding—there is only witnessing in silence. And Isaac marched forward with their ashes for the food he would eat, and with his drink intermingled with their tears, hoping for the day when those who committed such evil would drink the wine of God's fury, undiluted in his cup of retribution, in fire and brimstone, to be tortured in the presence of the holy angels and the smoke of their torture rise forever and ever.

And Elie watched in horror as old agricultural machines used to sort wheat from other grains were put into service to ventilate ashes from bodies in search of dental gold.

Jesus was witness, too. "The great dragon, the primeval serpent, known as the devil, who led all the world astray, has hurled down to earth and his angels of death have hurled down with him. Who can compare with the beast? Who can fight against him? The beast was allowed to mouth its boasts and blasphemies and to be active for forty-two months...It was allowed to make war against the saints...The beast compelled everyone—small and great alike, rich and poor, slave and citizen—to be branded on the right hand or forehead. And yet did You not take them and bring them forth out of the iron furnace, out of Egypt, to be unto You a people of inheritance? Did You not then refine them, not as silver, but in the furnace of affliction? Was that not enough?

"God, did you not teach that one may not slaughter an animal and her young the same day? Yet, we are being slaughtered, mothers and sons and daughters, together, in Your Presence. God, are You in the grave with the men and women and children and babies that are buried? God are you buried alive?"

These were the last words of Elie as he went into the "little red house," chamber of death, not knowing that the last train would leave Hungary in August 1944 and that the rest of the Hungarian Jews would be force marched toward Germany in November of that year.

Nor would Elie ever know that Eichmann's only regret was he left the job unfinished. He had hoped to wipe out all the Jews of Hungary. He carried this regret to his trial in Israel in 1961 and took it with him to the grave.

So the still small voice within Elie was silenced, forever. Like so many before, he had followed in the footsteps of Israel's children, the suffering servant, who had waited in repose and rest to be helped, believing that quietness and confidence would be their strength.

On April 10, 1945 the Nazis moved the remnant of twenty thousand emaciated, tormented, dehumanized, empty vessels from Buchenwald and blew it up. Would this Holocaust be the end of the line for the *Lamed-Vov*, the thirty-six Just Men of Jewish Tradition? Those people who are humble, merciful, forgiving and caring for others and each generation save the world for all of God's creations?

April 11th dawned and as the Nazis moved the last to the assembly place, whatever life remained in the inmates rebelled with guns and grenades.

And at six pm the Americans entered the gates of hell.

12

THE SACRIFICE ON THE ALTAR

Men are always murderers, and their calmness and generosity is the calmness of a well-fed animal, that knows itself out of danger.

~ Leonid Andreyev, *The Red Laugh*

Thousands of years before, Isaac had waited, bound to the altar. And he remembered the sacrifice of others. Isaac looked back on the sacrifice made by Adam and Eve—giving up Utopia. How Cain in his ignorance, sacrificed Abel. And God, in his anger sacrificed his people in a flood. He remembered the admonitions against child sacrifice and the sacrifice of Sodom and Gemorrah. He recalled the sacrifices at the Temple.

"Holy true Master, how much longer will you wait before you pass sentence and take vengeance for our death on the inhabitants of the earth? Do not abandon us for ever, for the sake of your name; do not repudiate your covenant, do not withdraw your favour from us, for the Sake of Abraham, your friend, of Isaac your servant, your holy one, with whom you promised to maintain your covenant, a covenant in perpetuity, to be His God and the God of his descendants after him. Lord we have become the least of all nations."

Paul: "Not all who are from Israel are Israel; not all who are Abraham's seed are his since it is not the children of the flesh who are God's children, but the children of the promise. What should we say then? That the gentiles, although they were not looking for saving justice, found it, and this was saving justice that comes of faith; while Israel, looking for saving justice by law-keeping, did not succeed in fulfilling the Law. And why? Because they were tying it to actions and not in faith. But the Law has found its fulfilment in Christ so that all who have faith will be justified. The Jews are not exempt from the retribution of God."

hitler: 'The Lord helps those who help themselves'—This is not only a very pious phrase, but a just one. For one cannot assume that God exists to help people who are too cowardly and too lazy to help themselves and think God exists only to make up for the weakness of mankind. He does not exist for that purpose. He has always, at all times, blessed only those who were prepared to fight their own battles. If a nation forgets itself as completely as the German nation did at that time of the First World War, if it thinks it can shake off all honour and all good faith, Providence can do nothing but teach it a hard and bitter lesson. But even at that time we were convinced that once our nation found itself again, once it again became industrious and honourable, once each individual German stood up for his nation first and not for himself, once he placed the interests of the community above his own personal interests, once the whole nation again pursued a great ideal, once it was prepared to stake everything for the ideal, the hour would come when the Lord would declare our traits at an end. I do not fear the verdict on our mentalities. Who are these egoists in other countries? Each one of them merely defends the interests of his class. Behind them all stands either the Jew or their money-grubbers."

Abraham, Isaac and Sarah cried out: "God of Vengeance, shine forth. Arise, judge of the world and give back the proud what they deserve. How long are the wicked, God, how long are the wicked to triumph? They bluster and boast, they flaunt themselves, all the evil-doers. They crush your people, God, they oppress your heritage; they murder the widow and the stranger and bring the orphan to a violent death."

It was so hard to believe that in the very heart of Europe, one of the oldest civilizations in the world that had been shaped by centuries of Christian religious thinking and by the Enlightenment, how quickly human beings could cease to be human. Yet, there was history. St John Chrysostom wrote of the Jews: "The synagogue is not only a whorehouse and a theatre; it is also a den of thieves and a haunt of wild animals...not the cave of a wild animal merely, but of an unclean wild animal...The Jews have no conception of things at all, but living for the lower nature, all agog for the here and now, no better disposed than pigs or goats, they live by the rule of debauchery and inordinate gluttony..."

And the serpent reveled in his words.

hitler: "There is one error which cannot be remedied once men have made it...the failure to recognize the importance of conserving the blood and the race free from intermixture and thereby the racial aspect and character which are God's gift and God's handiwork. It is not for men to discuss the question of why Providence created different races, but rather to recognize the fact that it punishes those who disregard its work of creation. As I look back...my first feeling is one of thankfulness to our Almighty God for having allowed me to bring this work to success. For I am the German messiah. I will save the nation, if only the citizenry will put its destiny in me. Only those who are of German blood can be considered as our fellow Germans regardless of creed. Hence a Jew cannot be regarded as a fellow German. The Jew is a parasite. Wherever he flourishes, the people die. Blood sin and desecration of the race are the original sin in this world and then the end of humanity which surrenders to it. I am acting in accordance with the will of the Almighty Creator; by defending myself against the Jew, I am fighting for the work of the Lord. Did not Paul IV say that it is absurd and inconvenient to the utmost degree that Jews, condemned for their faults by God to eternal slavery, can with the excuse of being protected by Christian love, be tolerated living among us? And did he not establish the ghetto in Rome to keep the Jews separate from the rest?"

Abraham, the father of all of us, the most righteous asks: "How to bless God? We are witness to thousands of children burning in pits: six crematories working night and day, on Saturdays and feast days; the creation of Auschwitz, Birkenau, Buna, and so many factories of death. How can we say Blessed art Thou, Eternal,

Master of the Universe, Who chose us among the races to be tortured day and night, to see our fathers, our mothers, our brothers and sisters end in the crematoria? I have seen how you tolerate those who sin and have spared those who do evil and have destroyed your own people...and have not shown anyone how your way may be understood...what nation has kept your commandments as well as Israel? How do we praise You who has allowed us to be butchered on Your altar?"

Isaac, trembling before God and all the angels, remembering how he felt, ready to be burned as a sacrifice to the God of his father, "We have become the burnt offering, the sacrifice, the oblation. I beseech you, my Lord, why have I been endowed with the power of understanding? For I did not want to ask about heavenly things, but about those things which we experience every day...why the people you loved have been given to godless tribes...and why we pass from the world like insects, and our life is like mist? The mephitic effluvia given off by the pyres have contaminated the surrounding countryside. The pitiful wails of people mourning for their children can be heard from far away. The stars overhead have lost their innocence. They have become sparks of the fire which devour us."

And they look to Paul who so long ago had said, "When the Lord Jesus appears from heaven with the angels of his power. He will come amid flaming fire; he will impose a penalty on those who do not acknowledge God and refuse to accept the gospel of our Lord Jesus. Their punishment is to be lost eternally, excluded from the presence of the Lord and from the glory of his strength—on that day when he comes to be glorified among his holy ones and marvelled at by all who believe in him."

Jesus: "I say that the Father loves the Son and has entrusted everything into my hands that through me the world might be saved. And I say anyone who believes in me has eternal life and anyone who refuses to believe in me will never see life: because God's retribution hangs over him. But I have never witnessed as much suffering as I have here; not from the beginning of the creation until now, never would I have foreseen such a sin as this. Why would God the Father allow these demonic forces and their arrogant human agents to overrun the world with apparent impunity?"

Was it possible that God, the Rock, the Redeemer had been distracted, for just a moment? Did He choose to turn His gaze away from His chosen people, the children He had redeemed from slavery, and taken out of Egypt to freedom, to look upon His universe? And was it in that moment, that quick glance away from His children, that evil covered the earth like molten lava?

Or was it the children of Babel who unleashed the unthinkable? Were they not the ones who turned their gaze away from the slaughter of innocents? Were they not the ones who refused shelter to the Lambs of God?

At midnight the red sky could be seen for miles; midnight, the hour when God Himself weeps over the destruction of the Temple. The Temple is His people.

Abraham, the one who challenged God when He chose to destroy Sodom and Gemorrah demands, "When You were deceived by Adam and Eve, You drove them out of Paradise. When Noah's generation displeased You, You brought the flood. When Sodom no longer found favour in Your eyes You made the sky rain down fire and sulphur. And though we are tortured, butchered, gassed and burned, and the sky is raining down fire and ash we still praise and bless You. How great is this sacrifice that You have made of your children, to save the others?"

Even the Jews of Rome, the oldest Diaspora in Western Europe, two thousand years old, living in the city before the Fisherman had arrived, were not safe from the onslaught. Under the sight of Pope Pius XII the Jews of Rome had been gathered into a ghetto on the banks of the Tiber and then on October 16, 1943 were dragged from their homes, loaded onto trucks and transported to the barracks of Collegio Militare, a half mile from the Vatican. But the Vatican did not interfere. Although pressed on all sides, the Pope did not allow himself to be drawn into any demonstration of reproof at the deportation of the Jews of Rome. The Jews of Rome were taken to the gas chambers of Auschwitz and Birkenau. More than one thousand Roman Jews were reduced to ashes.

Jesus, seeing the work of the red serpent all around him looked up to His Father and demanded that the followers of the beast, who branded the fallen be made to drink the wine of God's fury, fire and brimstone, in retribution for those who sent the saints up in smoke.

"When the time will come—and indeed it surely will—let the world read and know what the murderers perpetrated. Here, before You, is the richest material for the mourner when he writes the elegy for the present time. Here is the most powerful subject matter for the avenger...You are obligated to assist them, to help them, as they have paid with their own lives, which today are very cheap."

13

SOPHIA'S STORY

Their blood cries out, but their voice is stilled.

~ Gideon Hausner

The Einsatzgruppen was established by the Nazis to kill Jews in the Soviet Union. Three thousand men were divided into four groups. It is estimated that the Einsatzgruppen along with German armed forces and collaborators murdered about two million Jews.

The needs of the German people, their need for slave labour, were not nearly as important as the need to rid the land of all of its Jews. Orders came from Berlin that on the Jewish question, clarification should by now have been achieved through oral discussion. As a matter of principle, economic considerations should be overlooked in the solution of the problem. In 1942 General Alfred Jodl, Chief of the Army's Operation Staff, requested permission to hold on to the Jews until they could be replaced by other workers in order to continue with essential war work. This was not acceptable to the war machine—the war against the Jews. Steps must be ruthlessly taken against all those who think it is their business to intervene in the alleged interests of the war industry, but who in reality want only to support the Jews and their businesses. The few Jewish forced-labour concentration camps that were kept open were only to be temporary as hitler had clearly stated that even from there the Jews are some day to disappear. The needs of the military were not to get in the way of killing the Jews. It seemed that hitler, in his obsessive need to rid the world of the Jews, turned them into the sacrifice that saved the rest of Europe.

And while the whole world shone with the light of day and unhindered went about its work; over them alone there spread a heavy darkness, an image of the dark that would receive them. But heavier than the darkness was the burden they were to themselves.

Sophia, a young girl, curious, ambitious and cheerful, and all pretty in pink makes her way to the pit. She is wearing the dress her mother had made for her; a dress made from soft pink velvet cloth with white ruffles around the skirt and a white Peter-Pan collar. Her Bubbie had embroidered little pink petals with pale yellow centres around the white collar. She wore little white socks with pink dots and her special black shoes that she had worn only to synagogue on the Sabbath and festival days. Her dark, wavy hair was tied back with a clip that had an amethyst in the middle surrounded by baby seed pearls. It had been a gift from her mother on her last birthday—her sixth. Try as she may, a few strands of her hair always managed to escape from the clasp and form tiny wisps that framed her oval face. There was a matching amethyst ring that Sophia would receive on her tenth birthday.

She has the scent of innocence, like all little girls, so soft and sweet and gentle. As she made her way down the steps she was startled by a sound and turned around to see a man walking toward the pit. She thought she heard his name being called by those just behind him. She stretched her arm out to him, like a child to her father and beckoned him to come closer. As he drew near, she reached up on her tip toes. He bent down to her, as a father to a child, and she cupped her small hand around his ear and in a whisper, like the flutter of a butterfly's wings, she asked, "Is it true?"

"Is what true?"

"Are you really Jesus?"

"Yes I am. And who are you?"

"I am Sophia. I am told that my name means wisdom. Is it true what they say? Are you the messiah?"

"I am and you will see the Son of man seated at the right hand of the Power and coming with clouds of heaven."

"Are you the King of the Jews? Did you die and after three days rise again? And when you died, is it true that the earth quaked, the rocks were split, the tombs opened and the bodies of many holy people rose from the dead? I am asking because I am hoping that we will rise, too. See over there; that is my mother. She had such beautiful long black hair that she tied in a scarf. They shaved all of her hair. She was shot by that one, there. They call him Blobel. He uses Mausers to kill us. And there, my two little brothers. And there, my baby sister. All dead.

All around her the Einsatzgruppen were carrying on with their chores while in the background one could hear music. An interlude played by the Quartet for the End of Time. The sound of dissonance from a piano, a clarinet, a violin and a violoncello. It was beautiful and haunting. Sweet cascades of mournful chords: *weltschmerz*: A world of pain. You could imagine the descent of the seventh angel, at the sound of whose trumpet the mystery of God will be consummated, and who announces that there should be time no longer. How true for so many thousands. Their time ending, before their time, taking with them the time allotted for all those who should have come after them to all eternity. Past, present and future generations wiped out to the sound of a quartet. The sound of the harmonious silence of Heaven.

And so Sophia shared her story with this man. This man they called Jesus.

"We had all climbed into lorries. They drove us toward a forest where each truck unloaded fifty of us—mainly women and children. People who had been summoned from the villages brought their shovels. I watched as they dug huge graves. Sometimes mommies and daddies dug the pits. And when they had finished their work, the Gestapo began theirs. Everyone was lined up and sent into the pit to be shot. First they made everyone undress and the guards beat them; they ripped the gold teeth out of their mouths; completely naked families went down the steps into the pit and lay face down on the bodies of those who had already been shot. I saw one villager bring chlorine and ash to stop the blood from running out of the pits. I don't understand. There was such a thirst for Jewish blood. No one helped us. No one."

All found themselves on the edge of the deep and woeful pit that echoes with the moans of endless grief. Bestiality without end.

And Jesus wept as he repeated "Blessed are the poor, blessed are the gentle, blessed are those who mourn."

hitler, part of the group responded; "The Catholic Church considered the Jews pestilent for 1500 years, put them in ghettos because it recognized the Jews for what they were...I recognize the representatives of this race as pestilent for the state and for the church and perhaps I am thereby doing Christianity a great service."

Paul, cries out; "Do not fear. This stumbling will not lead to your final downfall. It's out of the question! On the contrary, you are bringing salvation for the gentiles. And if your fall proves a great gain to the gentiles, how much greater again will come when all is restored to you."

This was beyond Sophia's ability to understand. She was watching the death of her loved ones and thousands more. For what? She spoke of other methods of murdering her people.

"Sometimes my people had to walk to the trench and present their necks. See there—that is Humpel, a German policeman. He says that the priests told them that the Jews were the murderers of God so he walks on the dead bodies, pistol in hand and murders each Jew, one after the other with a bullet in back of neck. See the white coat he wears over his uniform—like a doctor's smock. I watched as he took regular breaks from his work had a small glass of liquor and then went back into the ditch to massacre another naked Jewish family. After each round of shootings the girls from the village had to go into the pit and push the bodies down with their feet like squishing grapes. Were they trying to turn blood into wine? They covered them with dirt so the next group could be shot on top. Without passion, without haste, they slaughtered us. Blood ran along the path after the shootings like the ever-flowing source of a river fouled with mingled blood and mud. Then they covered the pit with chalk to try and dry the ground."

The smell was putrid.

Paul: "We must remember that God's saving justice was witnessed by the Law and the prophets, but now it has been revealed altogether apart from the law. God's saving justice is given through faith in Jesus Christ to all who believe. No distinction is made. All have sinned and lack God's glory and all are justified by the free gift of his grace through being set free in Christ Jesus. God appointed him as a sacrifice for reconciliation, through faith by the shedding of his blood and so showed his justness; first for the past when sins went unpunished because He held his hand and now again for the present age to show He is just and justifies everyone who has faith in Jesus."

Isaac: "All are justified? Are you suggesting that these barbarians by accepting Jesus have been given the gift of grace? You can stand here in the stench and the excrement and burning bodies and say that all are justified; no distinction is made?

"If God sacrificed Jesus for the sins of the past and the present why is He standing by watching the shedding of the blood of His people? Are you suggesting that this would not be happening if the Jews had just accepted Jesus into their hearts? Are you suggesting that God is standing idly by, allowing His children to be cremated because they did not accept Jesus as the messiah? God admonished the angels for singing following the drowning of the Egyptians in the Sea of Reeds, but God would let the Nazis cremate us?"

What could Paul say?

hitler answered: "We will use that strength the Almighty has given us to use; that in it and through it we may wage the battle of our life. . .The others in the past years have not had the blessing of the Almighty—of Him who in the last resort, whatever man may do, holds in his hands the final decision. Lord God, let us never hesitate or play the coward, let us never forget the duty which we have upon us. . .We are all proud that through God's powerful aid we have become once more true Germans. It matters not whether these weapons of ours are humane; if they gain us our freedom, they are justified before our conscience and before God."

Sophia, walking shyly by the side of Jesus, carried on: "We, the children, we are being kept to the end."

Gratuitous terror.

"I have been watching and listening so I can bear witness, so that I can tell God. They tear the little ones from their mother's arms; throw them into the air to be used by the machine gunners as targets. That's what they did to my baby sister, Judith. She was shot while in the air. The soldiers had thrown her up and away, and then shot her as she fell to the ground. I heard her screaming, screaming, screaming and then she splattered onto the others and her screaming stopped.

"And the people. Watching. Mothers and fathers holding their children up high to see the killing of the Jews, to participate in the frenzy, clapping and cheering the whole time while the clothes of the Jews were torn and their hearts ripped apart. And some took pictures!

"They shoot old people and young children with the same emotion as swatting flies. The Germans throw grenades into the pit after shooting us because not all are dead. The Einsatzgruppen are well-trained for their work. And they have a great deal of experience. They have teenagers from the towns bring hemp and sunflowers to burn the bodies."

Sunflowers, while the ground and the rivers and springs of water turned to blood. We are drinking death as you drink water or air, mouth open, eyes closed, fingers clenched.

14

WHY HAVE YOU FORSAKEN US?

Then with knowledge of death as walking one side of me, And the thought of death close-walking the other side of me, And in the middle, as with companions, and as holding the hand of companions

~ Walt Whitman

hitler knew he was right. "Did not Eusebius say that certain people had to be eliminated from humanity like a poison, that they infect the whole world with great evil? And did not the great Constantine, the one who made Christianity the religion of the Roman Empire, declare that each person shall be free to worship as seems good to him and then state the Jews were to be included among the horde of evil-doers to be vanquished as he saw them as killers of prophets and murderers of the Lord? The Jew is in unclean dress, physical uncleanness. Jews are at the heart of everything that is diseased. The Jew is no German. We will carry on the struggle until the last Jew is removed from the German Reich. The solution to the Jewish question must be removal of the Jews from our nation, not because we would begrudge them their existence—we congratulate the rest of the world on their company—but 'We are God's people.'

"My feelings as a Christian point me to my Lord and Saviour as a fighter. It points me to a man who once in his loneliness, sur-rounded only by a few followers, recognized these Jews for what they were and summoned men to fight against them and who, God's truth! was greatest not as sufferer but as fighter. In boundless love as a Christian and as a man I read through the passage which tells us how the Lord rose in His might and seized the scourge to drive out of the Temple the brood of vipers and adders. How terrific was His fight for the world against the Jewish poison. I recognize more profoundly than ever before in the fact that it was for this that He had to shed His blood upon the Cross."

And Sophia listened, looking into the eyes of the man beside her whom hitler was describing as a hero.

hitler "We have faith that one day Heaven will bring the Germans back into the Reich over which there shall be no Soviet star, no Jewish Star of David but above the Reich there will be the symbol of German labour—the Swastika. I have been divinely chosen to lead the people into Germany's third kingdom, the Third Reich and bring Christ's thousand-year kingdom on earth."

Isaac could bear no more. "I have earned the right to defend my people. Did I not earn that right on Moriah? So I ask You, Lord, why do you allow this sinner to lurk for the chance to spill blood? Why did You not sacrifice me? Why did you not offer me up as a sacrifice—totally consumed by fire? Is it not said the murder of one is equal to the murder of all? If You had ended my life these children would not be in the furnace. Why did you not take me, just me? Why did you save me, one person, one child, and let millions of Your other children be murdered? Why did You let me live only to witness the children of my children perish in puffs of smoke, ashes blown in the wind, others shot to fall into the abyss, one on top of the other at the pleasure of those born of woman but children of Beelzebub? To what end?"

And his father Abraham, no one was ever his equal in glory, responded, "Lord, You promised me on oath to bless the nations through my descendants, to multiply me like the dust on the ground, to exalt my descendants like the stars, and to give them the land as their heritage. Let us see the nations suffer vengeance for shedding your servants' blood."

Paul: "And about Israel this is what Isaiah cried out: 'Although the people of Israel are like the sand of the sea, only a remnant will be saved; for without hesitation or delay the Lord will execute his sentence on the earth.'"

hitler: "I have often been a prophet in my life and was generally laughed at. During my struggle for power, the Jews primarily received with laughter my prophecies that I would someday assume the leadership of the state and thereby of the entire Volk and then among many other things, achieve a solution of the Jewish problem. I suppose that meanwhile the resounding laughter of Jewry in Germany is now choking in their throats."

Abraham, Sarah and Isaac cannot believe what they are hearing. Not again. "They are laying plans against Your people, conspiring against those You cherish; they say, 'Come, let us annihilate them as a nation, the name of Israel shall be remembered no more.'"

Hitler:"The Jew is the greatest obstacle to the fulfillment of this racial millennium. The mightiest counterpart to the Aryan is represented by the Jew. Whoever knows the Jew, knows the Devil. The vileness of the Jew is so gigantic that no one need be surprised if among our people the personification of the evil as a symbol of all evil assumes the living shape of the Jews. The war will not end as the Jews imagine, namely in the liquidation of all the European and Aryan peoples. The outcome of this war will be the extermination of Jewry. For the first time it will not be the other nations who will bleed to death. For the first time we will practice the ancient Jewish law: an eye for an eye, a tooth for a tooth."

Sophia, knowing that her end was near said ever so softly, so gently, "Yeshua, you used to be called Yeshua before they called you Jesus; Yeshua, do you think that God is sacrificing the Jews to save the world just as He sacrificed you? Is it true that there is no forgiveness save by blood? Will the death of my people act as forgiveness for the world?"

Jesus listens wordlessly, looking around him in the pit of the dead and the living dead. "I hear my brothers and sisters voices howling from the depths of the earth."

The moaning and groaning, the gasps, as the wretched try to claw their way through the bodies, the sand, the blood and urine and feces, to fight for one more breath. Finger nails torn off as hands scratched the earthen walls, desperately trying to get out, to find air, to breathe.

Here, in the pit, you could still hear the music of Messiaen's Angel, ever so faintly, announcing the end of Time with chords and melodies that are swords of fire.

The pits breathed for three days. It took three days of writhing and twisting, eternal tortures moaning and movement before the pit settled into silence. That's how long it took for all to die, suffocating under the bodies of others, covered in two to three metres of sand. Then, they would not cry out to the world again.

Sarah: "What did we ever do to them? Why do they hate us so much?"

Paul: "You killed the king of the Jews."

Abraham: "King of the Jews? There is only one King—Adonai, Elohenu, God of tenderness and compassion, slow to anger, rich in faithful love and constancy, maintaining his faithful love to thousands, forgiving fault crimes and sin, yet letting nothing go unchecked."

A hand suddenly came out of the pit and grabbed the foot of Jesus. And Jesus remembered. He closed his eyes and saw himself adorned with a crown of thorns, nailed to the cross. He could feel the sensation of suffocating slowly, nailed to the cross, unable to move. He remembered the feeling of smothering on the cross like the men women and children in the boxcars, in the pits, in the gas chambers. He remembered being stabbed in his abdomen by the Roman guards, his clothes torn asunder, "My God, my God, why have you forsaken us?"

And then Jesus, his hands lying gently on the head of Sophia, turned heavenward and cried, "Why God, why did you sacrifice me on the cross? Was I not sacrificed so that through me the world would be saved? Was I not the one man to die for the people, rather than that the whole nation should perish? Take pity on them, Master, Lord of the Universe, look at them, spread fear of Yourself throughout all other nations. Raise your hand against foreign nations and let them see Your might. As, in their sight, you have proved yourself holy to us, so now, in our sight, prove yourself great to them. Rouse your fury, pour out your rage, destroy the opponent, those ruthless murderers of children, those eaters of entrails, at feasts of human flesh and of blood, those initiates of secret brotherhoods, annihilate the enemy. Hasten the day, remember the oath and let people tell of your mighty deeds. Take pity, Lord, on the people called by your name, on Israel on whom you have made first born. Does salvation not come from the Jews?"

Isaac and Jesus watched as Sophia walked away from them, down the three steps, one, two, three, slowly disappearing into the pit, into the kingdom of the dead, to join all those who had entered before her. And accompanying her into the abyss were the sounds of the last strands of the last movement of Messiaen's cry to God; the music slowly ascending to the upper range of a violin and a piano, the notes painting the ascent to Paradise.

hitler had moved on. But hovering above was the mighty Angel who announces the end of Time, clothed with a cloud, and a rainbow upon his head. He stood with one foot on the sea and one foot on the earth. And in the air could be heard the trumpets of the Apocalypse.

On the last step, Sophia turned her head to gaze one more time at the man called the messiah and at Isaac, her bother in time. And as Sophia stood so silently, afraid but stoic, they saw behind her a multitude of shadows; shadows of all the souls who had come before her; her ancestors who bequeathed to her all that would have made her the woman she would have become: Adam and Eve; and Noah; Abraham and Sarah; Isaac and Rebecca; Jacob and Leah and Rachel; Joseph and Dina, Judah and Benjamin; Moses and Joshua; Deborah and Yael; Ruth and Naomi; Saul and David; Solomon the builder of the Temple; Elijah and Elisha; Esther; the Maccabees and Rabbis Hillel and Akiva; and the Jews who survived the Crusades and the Inquisition and the pogroms that it made possible for Sophia's mother and father to give her life; all descended into the pit with Sophia.

In her was found all the blood of the prophets and saints, and all the blood that was ever shed on earth. Now there will be no more;

Wisdom will be buried with Sophia until a time when wisdom can be resurrected. And it will be Wisdom who delivers this holy people, a blameless race, from a nation of oppressors.

Sarah, ravaged by the horrors of war, came upon the scene and mourned for her dead children and those never to be born: the death of all their music, symphonies, poetry, prose, artwork, stories; the loss of what could have been.

And what a loss it would be. In the 21st century there were only fourteen million Jews. That is approximately 0.2 percent of the world population. And yet, American Jews accounting for two percent of the American population accumulated 22% of all Nobel Prizes, 20% of all Field Medals for mathematics, 67% of the John Clarke Bates medals for economics under the age of forty. Jewish people won 38% of the Oscars for Best Director, 20% of the Pulitzer prizes for non-fiction and 13% of Grammy Lifetime Achievement Awards.

The Jewish eternal state of Israel, the phoenix risen from the ashes of evil, now a mere 70 years old in her modern reincarnation, has gone from a country of swamp and desert to a Start-Up nation, competing with America's Silicon Valley. From Mobileye alerting drivers of potential hazards, to Waze, the navigation app. From ReWalk assisting severely physically disabled to people walk, to Netafim revolutionizing agriculture with drip agriculture for water deprived areas. Israeli-designed GrainPro Cocoons provide a surprisingly simple and cheap way for African and Asian farmers to keep their grain market-fresh. Hebrew University's Prof. David Levy developed strains of potatoes that thrive in hot, dry climates, and can be irrigated by saltwater. From the 8088 processor, laying the foundations for the modern computer to the USB flash drive. From the PillCam, Capsule Endoscopy, the least invasive means of visualizing the small bowel to Water-gen LTD, a low-cost solution for creating a renewable source of fresh and clean drinking water by extracting it directly from the atmosphere. Then there is Copaxone originally developed by a doctor at the Weizmann Institute of Science in Rehovot, that is now the world's top-selling treatment for multiple sclerosis. And the Emergency Bandage, designed by an Israeli military medic to stop bleeding from hemorrhaging wounds caused by traumatic injuries in the field.

How much greater would their contributions have been if the Jews had not been sacrificed in the conflagration?

15

BUT WHERE IS GOD?

The neighborhood bully been driven out of every land,
He's wandered the earth an exiled man.
Seen his family scattered, his people hounded and torn,
He's always on trial for just being born.
He's the neighborhood bully.

~ Bob Dylan

The Israelites had always been proud of their ancestry. Perez was the father of Hezron. Hezron was the father of Ram. Ram was the father of Amminadab. Amminadab was the father of Nashon. Nashon was the father of Salmon. Salmon was the father of Boaz. And Boaz married Ruth, the Moabite, the widowed daughter-in-law of Naomi. Boaz was the father of Obed. Obed was the father of Jesse. And Jesse was the father of David. But the history of the six million would die with them. The past was past but the future was dead.

The extent of the loss, the wanton murder of the Jewish people was too much to bear. The sun refused to rise. The cherubim cowered under their wings unable to bear witness. And the sun turned into darkness and the moon into blood.

There were cries and noise, thunder and earthquakes, and disorder over the whole earth. But then, as from a little spring, there grew a great river, a flood of water. Light came as the sun rose and the humble were raised up and devoured the mighty. The war against the Jews ended.

And it was a war against the Jews more than anything else.

There had been a deliberate decision on the part of the National Socialist regime, even in the final stages of economic warfare, to liquidate the Jews rather than exploit them towards obvious productive and financial ends. The diversion of resources from the

Nazi war effort to the Final Solution may have been a factor in the defeat of hitler and his forces by the Allies.

Himmler "All in all we have carried out this heaviest of our tasks in a spirit of love for our people. In our history, this is an unwritten and never-to-be-written page of glory." By this time more than five million Jews had been erased from the earth in gas chambers and by bullets. Three hundred thousand Jews had been brutally massacred in the Vilna regions and Lithuania Kaunas. Ultimately 1.5 to 2 million Jews, men, women, children, the sick, and the weak, the elderly were annihilated from a Holocaust by bullets, by the Einsatzgruppen and other units of the security police. Thirty thousand Jews were murdered in Lvov; 15,000 Jews were murdered in Stanislawow; 5,000 Jews were murdered in Tarnapol; 2,000 Jews were murdered in Zlocwow; 4,000 Jews were murdered in Brzezany.

There had been in Germany and Austria and throughout all of Europe and the Americas, across Asia and Russia, to Australia and Africa an *ignorantia affectata,* a cultivated ignorance, a willful lack of knowledge regarding the extermination of the Jews and a concerted effort to avoid rescuing the Jews of Europe.

The west had been quite prepared to sacrifice the Jews in order to free the Allies for other more important work. President Roosevelt who held back the bombing of Auschwitz had had no problem diverting manpower to save the artistic and historic monuments in Europe. Nor did he have a problem with Allied ships being diverted to bring thousands of Muslims on a religious pilgrimage to Mecca in 1943. Cavendish Cannon, a State Department official opposed rescuing Jews for fear they would want to come to the West and like so many others, he, too, viewed the Jews as a burden and a curse. His colleague Robert Alexander opposed rescuing Jews on the grounds that it would take the burden and the curse off hitler. And even General George Patton managed to divert U.S. troops to rescue 150 of the prized Lipizzaner dancing horses in Austria, in April 1945. But bombing Auschwitz? That would require diverting the bombers away from the oil tanks. Saving Jews was not a priority. And hitler was well aware from the time of the Wannsee Conference on January 20, 1942 that the world did not want her Jews.

Thus it often happened to those placed in authority, that having entrusted friends with the conduct of affairs and allowed themselves to be influenced by them, they find themselves sharing with them the guilt of innocent blood and involved in irremediable misfortunes. Look what is before you at the crimes perpetrated by a plague of unworthy officials. While the wicked supposed they had a holy nation in their power, they themselves lay prisoners of the dark, in the fetters of the long night, confined under their own roofs, banished from the eternal providence. While they thought to remain unnoticed with their secret sins, curtained by dark forgetfulness...

So often the question is asked: "Where was God?"

Nietzsche had an answer. "Whereto has gone God?" he cried. I shall tell you, he said. "We have slain him—you and I! All of us are his murderers! But how have we done this? How had we the means to drink the sea dry? Who gave us a sponge to efface the entire horizon? What were we about when we uncoupled this earth from its sun? Away from all suns? Are we falling continu-ously? And backward and sideways and forward in all directions? Is there still an above and a below? Are we not wandering lost as though as through an unending void? Does vacant space not breathe at us? Has it not grown colder? Is there not perpetual nightfall and more night? Must we not light lanterns in the morning? Do we hear nothing of the noise in the gravediggers who are burying God? Is there no smell of divine putrefaction?—the gods also decompose! God is dead! God stays dead. And we have killed him! How shall we comfort ourselves, who are killers above killers? The holiest and the mightiest that the world has hither to possessed has bled to death under our knives—who shall wipe that blood off us?"

But God was there; crying, His tears falling to His altar. The Holy Spirit fleeing to the Wailing Wall to mourn the millions of souls shattered into innumerable pieces, now sparks of the cosmos. God was waiting, hoping, praying that the people would remember and abide by His teachings. He is always waiting for the righteous to return. One not afraid to die for speaking truth. A moral and ethical child of God. Who will it be? When will that righteous one appear? The Lord will come out of his place to punish the inhabitants of the earth for their iniquity. Then the blood shall be wiped off and we will once again reach for the Seraphim and turn away from the call of the wild.

16

PASSED DOWN FROM ONE HAND TO ANOTHER

Write this down in a book to commemorate it, and repeat it over to Joshua, for I shall blot out all memory of Amalek under heaven. God will be at war with Amalek generation after generation.

~ Exodus 17:14

The Nazis left the world a memorial to their folly so their offences could not pass unnoticed. In witness against whose evil ways a desolate land still smokes, where plants bear fruit that never ripens, where a monument to an unbelieving soul, there stands a pillar of salt. The earth disclosed her blood and no more covered her slain.

It was a lonely priest who walked the overgrown fields behind the little villages; fields that at one time had been the most luscious landscapes with the scent of fertile fields, covered in dew from heaven. They had had the richness of the earth filled with an abundance of wine and grain. Not anymore. The priest walking along the same paths of those now lost but not forgotten, looked down on a mound of earth, a gentle hill and there, poking out of the ground, a bone, a bone from the bones of the assassinated Jews. A bone of a child's shoulder blade here and a broken femur there; mixed with the bones of the sick cows and sheep that had inhabited the field before the human bones were thrown in. And here, the lonely priest, now on his knees, crying, reached out for the broken bones and felt the horror still living in them.

And He set me down in the midst of the valley, a valley full of bones. He made me walk up and down and all around. There were vast quantities of these bones on the floor of the valley; and they were very, very dry. He said to me "Son of man can these bones live?" Dry bones; hear the word of the Lord. The Lord says this to these bones. "I will bring a spirit into you and you will live. And I will lay sinews upon you and bring up flesh upon you, and draw over you a skin, and put a spirit in you and you shall live and you will know that I am the Lord."

There was a sound and there was a rustling noise and the bones came together, bone to its bone. There were sinews upon them and the flesh came up and the skin was drawn over them but there was no spirit. From the four winds, come O spirit, and breathe into these slain ones that they may live. These bones are the whole house of Israel. They say; Dried are our bones and lost is our hope. We are quite cut off. Behold I will open your graves, and I will cause you to come out of your graves, O my people, and I will bring you into the land of Israel.

And on that day, the Lord with his cruel and great and strong sword will punish Leviathan, the fleeing serpent, Leviathan, the twisting serpent, and he will kill the dragon that is in the sea.

The Lord will not be slow nor will He be dilatory on behalf of those now turned into ash, until He has crushed the loins of the merciless and exacted vengeance on the nations, until He has eliminated the hordes of the arrogant and broken the sceptres of the wicked, until He has repaid all the people as their deeds deserve and human actions as their intentions merit.

"And God shall wipe away all tears from their eyes; and there shall be no more death, neither sorrow, nor crying, neither shall there be any more pain: for the former things are passed away."

One would have the right to believe that the Jews sacrificed by fire would save the lives of those who remained and those who would follow as Jacob had been sent ahead down into Egypt to later save the Jewish people. But alas, evil was not yet finished with the Jewish people; the people who gave to the world an ethic of compassion.

Out of the quiet of the night, when evil finds comfort, a hissing sound rumbled beneath the dirt, a hand was seen; clutching a slightly torn and rumpled document dated 4:00 AM, April 29, 1945. "Above all I charge the leaders of the nation and those under them to scrupulous observance of the laws of race and to merciless opposition to the universal poisoner of all peoples, international Jewry."

It was the suicide note held by the author, adolf hitler. Wrapped around his hand were the hands of Amalek entwined in the coil of the hissing red serpent, the red thread held victoriously in his mouth all being pulled up by the hand of Haj Amin al-Husseini, the Grand Mufti of Jerusalem; the heir to hitler's accomplishments, a hero who fought the Jews with the help of hitler and Germany. He would carry forward with the war against the Jews, to bring to fruition the anti-Jewish war of extermination initiated by the Nazis.

Amin Al-Husseini, the Mufti would continue the struggle. Would the world turn away again as another tribe set out to destroy the Jews in another attempt to sacrifice the Jews for world peace?

17

HITLER NEED NOT FEAR

National Socialism could not have come to power in Germany if it had not found, in broad strata of the population, soil prepared for its sowing of poison. It is not accurate to say that the high military or the great industrialists alone bear the guilt.

~ Dr. Konrad Adenauer, following the Shoah

The world woke up and questioned their years of being wilfully blind, deaf and dumb. There was repentance and penance. Chest beating and flagellation. And the Jews were welcomed back to Europe and able to return to their homeland of 3500 years: Israel. For it is written that those who do God's work in this world must endure misery and humiliation waiting long and hard for their vindication. God will compensate His people for their sacrifice. The reward for the righteous may be long delayed, but it will not be denied. The world was at last at peace—with its Jews. Israel blossomed under the hands of her people while all around remained desert.

Sadly, though, we have not yet learned the greatest duty of the heart as Bahya Ben Joseph taught centuries ago "What is that which is greater than sin? Pride and hypocrisy."

The Shoah was not enough to stop the cascade of hate for the people who gave the ethic of compassion to the world. It is too difficult to follow: to hold back from acting on our baser instincts of lust and vengeance; might over right. It is far easier to oppress the upright man who is poor and not spare the widow, nor respect old age, white haired with many years. It is far easier to use might as the yardstick of right since weakness argues its own futility. Let us lay traps for the upright man, since he annoys us and opposes our way of life, reproaches us for our sins against the Law...We see him as a reproof to our way of thinking, the very sight of him weighs our spirits down...Let us test him with cruelty and with torture. In order to follow the teachings from The Book, one must diminish oneself as God diminished Himself (*Tzimtzum*), to make room for His children. A difficult task, for evil refuses to rest in its pursuit of sin.

Yet, how are we to recognize Satan? Eve stood right beside him and did not know the Evil she was embracing. Once recognized and acknowledged there is hope for repentance and redemption. But what of those who come face to face with the serpent and choose to ignore what is right in front of their eyes?

And then, beyond belief, there is once again a strange scent in the air. Is it a whiff of wilful blindness or a gust of evil intention? What was that sound? That rumble, that grumble, that chant, that rant, that rose over the hills and down into the valleys, across the desert and over the oceans.

"The Jews, the Jews, death to the Jews. Kill the parasites of the universe, an impudent people who used Muslim and Christian blood for their holy services in Passover. Destroy the Jews like sick dogs."

The sound of hatred against the Jews arose once again from the ashes; from Islam. For 100 years the West was made ready. The Muslim Brotherhood, a worldwide Islamist organization founded in Egypt in 1928 by Hassan al-Banna sought from its birth to implement Sharia-based governance globally. Its motto:

"Allah is our objective, the Prophet is our leader, the Qur'an is our law, jihad is our way, dying in the way of Allah is our highest hope."

The Muslim Brotherhood and all of its offshoots have planted themselves in the West with the intent to destroy the culture. The Brotherhood is the mothership for the Muslim Student Association formed in 1963, the Council on American-Islamic Relations (CAIR), the Islamic Society of North America (ISNA), the Islamic Association of Palestine founded in 1981 and Hamas founded by the Brotherhood in 1987. Other organizations have been developed to spread the word including; The United Association for Studies and Research, The Occupied Land Fund and the Media Office. ICNA's charitable arm, ICNA (Islamic Circle of North America) Relief, is a donor to the Al-Khidmat Foundation, a Pakistani JI (Jamaat-e-Islam) charity that, according to JI's own website, openly funds the Gaza-based terrorist group, Hamas.

We know their intent. In 2004 Federal investigators in the USA found "An Explanatory Memorandum on the strategic Goal for the Group in North America," May 22, 1991, in the home of Ismael Elbarasse, a founder of the Dar Al-Hijrah mosque in Falls Church, Virginia. Elbarasse was a member of the Palestine Committee, which the Muslim Brotherhood had created to support Hamas in the United States. This memorandum, derived from the general strategic goal of the Group in America which was approved by the Shura Council and the Organizational Conference in the year 1987 is "Enablement of Islam in North America, meaning: establishing an effective and a stable Islamic movement led by the Muslim Brotherhood..."

Saudi wealth had helped to spread the Muslim Brotherhood ideology globally beginning in the 1960's. "The Ikhwan [Muslim Brotherhood] must understand that their work in America is a kind of grand jihad in eliminating and destroying Western civilization from within and 'sabotaging' its miserable house by their hands and the hands of the believers so that it is eliminated and God's religion made victorious over all other religions."

To complete that task they began to spread fear of criticizing Islam and the Prophet. No greater crime could there be than criticizing the ideology of Islam. They call it Islamophobia; the irrational fear of Islam. The Organisation of Islamic Cooperation reached out to media, academics, and experts and engaged with Western governments to raise awareness, support the efforts of Muslim civil society bodies in the West, and engage all in developing plans and programs to counter Islamophobia. It remains a propaganda success; silencing critics; suppressing free speech.

This was not a new concept. Islamophobia had been promoted by the Nazis. The serpent had done his job. The lesson had been learned well.

Throughout the war years, the Nazi Propaganda Ministry repeatedly instructed the press to promote a positive image of Islam, urging journalists to give credit to the "Islamic world as a cultural factor." Goebbels in the autumn 1942 instructed magazines to discard negative images of Islam, which had been spread by church polemicists for centuries, and instead to promote an alliance with the Islamic world, which was described as both anti-Bolshevik and anti-Jewish. References to similarities between Jews and Muslims, as manifested in the ban of pork and the ritual of circumcision, were to be avoided. In the coming months, the Propaganda Ministry decreed that magazines should depict the U.S. as "the enemies of Islam" and stress American and British hostility toward the Muslim religion."

In 1941, the Wehrmacht distributed the military handbook *Der Islam* to train the troops to behave correctly towards Muslim populations.

Heinrich Himmler while expressing disdain for Christianity, found Islam "very admirable."

"What is there to separate the Muslims in Europe and around the world from us Germans? We have common aims. There is no more solid basis for cooperation than common aims and common ideals. For 200 years, Germany has not had the slightest conflict with Islam." The Nazis had found commonality with Islam.

But the words of hitler mattered most. All could take heart from his praise of Islam as the thread passed from one creed to another providing a bridge between two hateful ideologies. Islam for hitler was a *Männerreligion*; a religion of men; and hygienic too.

He had spoken of soldiers of Islam receiving a warrior's heaven, a real earthly paradise with houris and wine flowing. Islam, he had intoned, was a cult which glorifies the heroism and which opens up the seven Heavens to bold warriors alone. One could hear his lamentations; if only the Germans had been Muslims they would have conquered the world. Islam, he claimed, was much more suited to the 'Germanic temperament' than the Jewish filth.

In the last months of the war while hitler hid in his bunker he lamented that the Third Reich's efforts to mobilize the Muslim world had not been strong enough. "All Islam vibrated at the news of our victories," and Muslims had been "ready to rise in revolt."

But hitler need not have feared. Haj Amin al-Husseini worked to unite the Arabs with the Nazis, economically and ideologically, in an anti-Jewish Islamic movement across India to Central Europe and on to the Middle East.

And so the *Männerreligion* carried on without hitler.

"We the Palestinian nation, our fate from Allah is to be the vanguard in the war against the Jews until the resurrection of the dead, as the prophet Muhammad said: 'The resurrection of the dead will not arrive until you will fight the Jews and kill them...' We the Palestinians are the vanguard in this undertaking and in this campaign, whether or not we want this...

"Oh, our Arab brethren...Oh, our Muslim brethren...Don't leave the Palestinians alone in the war against the Jews...even if it has been decreed upon us to be the vanguard...Jerusalem, Palestine and Al Aksa (The Temple Mount), the land that Allah blessed and its surrounding areas will remain at the center of the struggle between Truth and Falsehood, between the Jews and the non-Jews on this sacred land, regardless of how many agreements are signed, regardless of how many treaties and covenants are ratified. For the Truth is in the Koran, as verified by the words of the prophet Muhammad that the decisive battle will be in Jerusalem and its environs: 'The resurrection of the dead will not occur until you make war on the Jews...'

"The battle with the Jews will surely come...the decisive Muslim victory is coming without a doubt, and the prophet spoke about in more than one Hadith and the Day of Resurrection will not come without the victory of the believers the Muslims over the descendants of the monkeys and pigs the Jews and with their annihilation."

"Oh Allah, accept our martyrs in the highest heavens. . .

Oh Allah, show the Jews a black day. . .

Oh Allah, annihilate the Jews and their supporters. . .

Oh Allah, raise the flag of Jihad across the land."

"Our battle with World Jewry. . .is a question of life and death. It is a battle between two conflicting faiths, each of which can exist only on the ruins of the other."

"When the Jews are wiped out. . .the sun of peace would begin to rise on the entire world."

And there, huddled under the prayer shawl, the blue thread of heaven woven through it, were Abraham and Sarah and Isaac. Not again. Not again. History repeating itself.

18

HAS THE OLD NOT BECOME NEW AGAIN?

And in the naked light I saw
Ten thousand people, maybe more
People talking without speaking
People hearing without listening
People writing songs that voices never share
And no one dared
Disturb the sound of silence.

~ Paul Simon

The serpent, who was possessed of great capabilities of speech and reasoning used to acquire power; gifts he uses as weapons of destruction, was not yet done. So sly was the serpent that he lay in wait until he found a man worshipped and revered by millions, not only in America, but around the world. A man whose election to the highest position; President, symbolized a new America, a better America, where there was real hope for change, putting racism in its place.

No antisemitism for him. Anti-Zionism was more to his taste. It was the esteem in which he was held that made it possible for this Amalek to attack Israel. Starting with his apology tour of the Middle East with the false idea that his words would stop the rise of Islamic terror and bring democracy to the Muslim countries; constantly pushing Israel for a return to indefensible borders in the name of a peace process that would bring another Islamic *Judenrein* state into the world; and meddling in Israel's elections, in his desire to bring in a president of Israel who would follow his lead.

But it was his last act regarding Israel that made it known to all that the red thread had firmly implanted in this man. For the first time in the history of the relationship between the America and

Israel, this President of the United States of America refused to stop a resolution against Israel made by the United Nations Security Council; Resolution 2334, one of more than seventy five resolutions against the Jewish State that declared Jewish communities in Judea/Samaria as illegal, Jerusalem the capital of Israel for thousands of years, no longer the Jewish capital, the Wailing Western Wall, where Jews for generations cried over the destruction of the Great Second Temple while praying for its rebuilding, no longer a Jewish place, putting Israel, the only democracy in the Middle East, the people who gave the world the ethic that underpins all democracies, at risk.

It was on that day, December 23, 2016, that the sun remained low in the eastern sky, on the cusp of the horizon, fearful of the coming days, for surely the world had lost its way.

This polished, silver-tongued, self-appointed false messiah, had spent his last days, his last breath as President, trying to destroy the Jewish state. A modern state that had survived three wars from Muslim states in their never-ending desire to annihilate the Jews, decades of terror attacks and then the attacks against her through the United Nations. He became the 21st century Amalek and his name will be put on the list of others that the Jewish people were taught to "Remember to Forget."

But this modern day Amalek had already entered into a deal with the devil. July 14, 2015 he, along with the leaders of the United Nations Security Council (oh, the irony of that name) China, France, Russia, United Kingdom, the United States, plus Germany along with the European Union signed a treaty with the devil; the Khamenei of Iran, giving him billions of dollars, in small bills, a "blood offering" to those who called for Death to Israel and Death to the West. That money went to sponsor terror. Had not this President already stated his preference for the Muslim Brotherhood in Egypt, a declared terrorist organization?

With the red thread in hand, he had forgotten or ignored the most important lesson from a true statesman from the past;

Winston Churchill: "An appeaser is one who feeds a crocodile hoping it will eat him last."

He was not alone. Is evil ever solitary?

The serpent knew he would be welcome in Iran. There he found the Khamenei and Hassan Rouhani, President of Iran, screaming for the destruction of Israel. Now, close your eyes. Listen. Can you hear it? Can you hear the chants and the rants of hundreds of thousands of Muslims on the streets?

"Death to Israel."

"Death to the Jews."

And the smell. What is that?

It is the smell of Israeli and American flags burning: death to the West.

The media and institutions of higher learning are just as infected. Echoes of the hatred for Jews from German professors reverberate through time. Accusations of Israel as an apartheid state on par with South Africa; calls for Boycott Divest and Sanction of the only democracy in the Middle East, are heard across University campuses around the world where antisemitism is on the rise from the left as well as the right. Universities like McGill, McMaster, York and Ryerson in Canada to UC Davis, New York University and Columbia in America, Exeter and Oxford in Britain and a rise in Jew hatred across Germany where the sales of hitler's Mein Kampf are rising astronomically.

And again in the churches; the same holy places that turned a blind eye to the death camps in Europe, now support BDS: The Anglican Church in Britain; the Pentecostal Appeal promoting the view that Israel is an apartheid state and is eradicating the history of the Arabs; the Mennonite Church USA; the Presbyterian Church; USA; the Church of Scotland; the United Church of Canada and the Latin Patriarchate of Jerusalem. And then there is Spain, home of the Inquisition, the burning of Jews before all Jews were expelled, has more than eighty towns joining the BDS of Israel.

Holocaust denial is a new form of Jew hatred, and the serpent is well aware. It is spread in Conferences like those taking place in

Iran where calls for Death to the Jews are normal. There are the attempts to make anti-Zionism separate from antisemitism as if calling for the eradication of the only Jewish state is acceptable. These calls come from organizations like Students for Justice for Palestine and the Muslim Student's Association, the Muslim Brotherhood and Council on American-Islamic Relations (CAIR).

Non-governmental organizations (NGO) Amnesty International Human Rights Watch, the Paris-based FIDH (the International Federation of Human Rights), Sabeel, Kairos Palestine, Electronic Intifada, have strayed into antisemitism.

World leaders, from Europe to America, from Vice-President Federica Mogherini of the European Union to Jeremy Corbyn and his Labour Party in Great Britain, Linda Sarsour, Rashida Tlaib and Ilhan Omar in America, Swedish PM Sven Lofven and his Foreign Minister, Margot Wallstrom; Ireland's President Michael Daniel Higgins and Minister of Foreign Affairs Simon Carbery Coveney, following his lead, all condemned Israel when given the opportunity.

So, too, did the leaders of the United Nations condemn Israel, the only democracy in the Middle East and North Africa, under attack more often than any other country including Muslim countries where gays are murdered and women are abused. Places like Syria, where Assad dropped gas on his own people, and North Korea where the people live in constant fear and poverty. And China, Russia, Myanmar, Turkey, Venezuela and Cuba. Resolutions against Israel come from UN Human Rights Council, UNESCO, World Health Organization and UN Nations General Assembly.

There are Muslim leaders who call for death to Jews from their mosques: Imam Raed Saleh Al-Rousan from Houston; Imam, Ammar Shahin in Davis, California; Sheikh Mahmoud Harmoush spoke out in his mosque in Riverside, California; Imam Ahmedul Hadi Sharif, Tennessee; Sheikh Ramadan Elsabagh, in Garland, Texas; Abdullah Khadra Raleigh, North Carolina; Sheikh Wael Al-Ghitawi, Montreal; Imam Mohamed Tatai Toulouse, France; Abu Bilal Ismail, an imam at the Grimhøj Mosque in Aarhus, Denmark.

The serpent was not done, though. Slithering forward in time it also found its way to Louis Farrakhan, the American leader of the Nation of Islam. Here was someone echoing the familiar. Bringing the horrors of the past into the present. No antisemite was he. Oh no, he was anti-termite.

He preached as leader of the Nation of Islam in America.

"Hitler is a very great man."

"And don't you forget, when it's God who puts you in the ovens, it's forever!"

"Satanic Jews have infected the whole world with poison and deceit."

"And you do with me as is written, but remember that I have warned you that Allah will punish you. You are wicked deceivers of the American people. You have sucked their blood. You are not real Jews, those of you that are not real Jews. You are the synagogue of Satan, and you have wrapped your tentacles around the U.S. government, and you are deceiving and sending this nation to hell. But I warn you in the name of Allah, you would be wise to leave me alone. But if you choose to crucify me, know that Allah will crucify you."

"The false Jew will lead you to filth and indecency."

"I know they stoned Jesus. I know they've killed the prophets of God there."

What caught the eye of the serpent, though, was the Democrat Party in America where he could see his own reflection. This was too good to be true. His thread wound round and round. Democrat Congressmen did not disavow him. Instead there rose a coalition of the KKK and Islamic antisemitism. David Duke endorsing Ilhan Omar, the promoter of the old shibboleths and canards about Jews and money, Jews and world dominance, Jews and dual loyalties. There she was protected by the Congressional Black Caucus, followers of Farrakhan. And there, too is Rashida Tlaib, a serial purveyor of antisemitism. And when the leadership of that party, including Bernie Sanders, Kamala Harris and Elizabeth Warren, was faced with the proof of Jew hatred, the party demurred and appeased their new left leaders.

Social media, from Facebook to Twitter, Instagram to YouTube, has aided the Jew-hating frenzy sharing information around the world in a nano-second. Now we know how much worse it would have been in the Nazi era.

Has the old not become new again?

As happened in Germany in the 20th century, Jew hatred has once again been normalized with a universal race to hate the lambs of God.

The great story of David and Goliath in the Israeli Valley of Elah has been perverted.

How is it possible for the table to have been laid again, the fields to be plowed just so for the flourishing of such hate? Yet the hatred for the Jews and now the Jewish State flourishes most in the followers of Islam, the resurrected Amalekites who learned well from their Nazi teachers and the followers of the now-dead Mufti; who wanted nothing less than the death of the Jews—the destruction of the Jewish state.

For is it not written in the hadith that the Prophet (blessings and peace of Allah be upon him) said:

"The Hour will not begin until you fight the Jews, until a Jew will hide behind a rock or a tree, and the rock or tree will say: 'O Muslim, O slave of Allah, here is a Jew behind me; come and kill him.'"

What is this persistent malevolence toward this people?

And so a new generation, raised on the presentation of hitler as one who performed a positive service to humanity by killing the Jews because they "spread destruction all over the world," shared its dreams about the end of the Jews in publications like the PLO youth magazine *Zayzafuna* funded by the Palestinian Authority.

I had a dream, said she.

"One hot day, I was very tired after a hard day. . .and suddenly I saw four white doors in front of me. I opened them in no particular order.

I opened the first door and saw a beautiful place full of flowers. I was surprised to see a man there. I asked him, 'Who are you?'

He said, 'I am Al-Khwarizmi.' [Ninth century Persian mathematician who lived in Baghdad, known for his contribution to the development of algebra.]

I said: 'You're the one who invented mathematics and arithmetic?' He said: 'Yes. What's your situation like today?'

I said: 'The Arabs and Muslims are in a deep sleep; they can't do anything. They have moved away from all the sciences.'

He [Al-Khwarizmi] said: 'Yes, I know that. The day will come when the Arabs will return to their glory. And you—you have a great duty, which is to take an interest in the Islamic sciences and to protect them from being forgotten.'

I said, 'I promise,' and left the door.

I turned to the next door; there hitler awaited me. I said, 'You're the one who killed the Jews?'

He [hitler] said: 'Yes. I killed them so you would all know that they are a nation which spreads destruction all over the world. And what I ask of you is to be resilient and patient, concerning the suffering that Palestine is experiencing at their hands.'

I said [to hitler]: 'Thanks for the advice.'

Then I turned to the third door, and met Naguib Mahfouz [Nobel Prize-winning Egyptian author], who was the one who knew best the value of time and how to use it.

He said: 'People's pastime, these days, has become killing time and wasting it, as though they are punishing themselves. So strive to use your time in the best way.'

At the fourth door I meet Saladin Al-Ayoubi [Muslim leader who defeated the Christian crusaders and conquered Jerusalem in the twelfth century].

He said: 'I am Saladin.'

I said: 'You were the one who liberated Jerusalem and Al-Aqsa [Mosque].'

He answered: 'Yes.'

I said: 'Return, oh Saladin, for Jerusalem and Palestine cry out and no one answers.'

He [Saladin] said: 'I know, but every time has its men, and the right man to liberate Jerusalem is still to come.'

And before I could finish my dream, the alarm clock rang and I woke up. It was seven in the morning, and I needed to go to school early, because I had promised Naguib Mahfouz that I would use time well."

Today, and every day, at least five times a day, she will recite Surah (chapter) al Fatiha ("The Opening") the first chapter of the Koran.

"I seek refuge in Allah from Satan the accursed. In the name of Allah the Beneficent, the Merciful. Not the path of those who have incurred Your anger (The Jews) or the path of those who have deviated (Christians), who have fallen astray."

Is it not beyond belief, post Holocaust, that pundits, professors, politicians and people of the cloth once again choose silence? How is it possible they have so quickly forgotten the scream of Martin Niemöller: "Who will speak for me?" Have we not yet learned that silence is collusion?

The Eternal will be at war against Amalek throughout the ages for these cowardly attacks on His people.

EPILOGUE

And so the whirling dervish winds of insanity once again careened across the land carrying within the dust of hate. But we find that the Jews marked out for annihilation are not criminals; they are in fact governed by most just of laws. They are the children of the Most High, the great and living God to whom we and our ancestors owe the continuing prosperity of our realm.

God, Himself, will send an angel before you to guard you as you go, to bring you to the place that He has prepared. Give him reverence and listen to all that he says, as he speaks the mighty Word from the heart of the fire.

The peals of thunder came from the silence accompanied by flashes of lightning, and then, before them, a dense cloud appeared on the mountain top followed by the piercing trumpet blast from the lips of the Archangel Michael whom God had put in charge of the entire liturgy of heaven and earth. They were all there, together to "Hear, O Israel" as the blast called out the evil one in their midst, to be hanged, a fitting punishment, which God, Master of the Universe will speedily inflict upon him.

And so it came to pass that the two great dragons came forward, each ready for the fray, and setting up a great roar. At the sound of them every nation made ready to wage war against the nation of the just. A day of darkness and gloom, of affliction and distress, oppression and great disturbance on earth! The entire upright nation was thrown into consternation at the fear of the evils awaiting it and prepared for death crying out to God.

Then, from its cry, as from a little spring, there grew a great river, a flood of water. Like Jacob who wrestled and prevailed over the angel, to be rewarded with the new name Israel, the Jewish people, Israel, continue the battle.

Then from the east there came a light as the sun rose and the humble were raised up and devoured the mighty, and sons and daughters of Jacob though wounded, rose again. Then Wisdom,

Sophia, came forth from the mouth of the Most High and covered the earth like a mist emanating a light to deliver this holy people, a blameless race, from a nation of oppressors.

Will the red thread retreat once again? If so, how deep, we do not know. But we do know only too well, the history that tends to repeat itself tends to be the history that reveals the lesser of our natures.

How will it end for the messengers of compassion?

The book is not yet closed.

AFTERWORD

I saw the face of evil, today. On my street. In a rural area of Ontario. He was going for a walk with his daughter. He lives in a tiny, beautiful village, five minutes away.

I was walking my dog and heard this conversation about education. And as I am wont to do, I went over and started talking. I love to talk to all the different people who come by here. All races, colours, creeds and I assume sexual orientation.

As we got to talking, my antenna started to poke up on the back of my head. This conversation was turning to a place I knew was not going to be good. He didn't. Now, the face of evil is tricky. Because evil can hide behind any face, anywhere, at any time. And sadly, we rarely realize we are standing beside evil as it happens.

We started talking about the Bible and he told me his views about people who believe the Bible, and we joked about the Ark that has been built as a replica from the Biblical description. I was joking with him about God being behind the Big Bang. But I knew this was going south.

He proudly shared his views about the west. Not fond of western values. Thinks the west is terrible—oppressors and all. And slowly it turned to. . .Israel. The Zionists. Those oppressors. Now, I am well trained in the facts about Israel. I write about Israel all the time. I am on the board of Hasbara. But, so what. When you stand beside evil, facts don't matter. Ever. And perhaps that is what we forget. Evil has no need for facts.

He went on about Trump, that Zionist. He attacked Christian Zionists for standing with Israel. There was venom in the air. A serpent had risen.

It was at that point that I mentioned that I am a Zionist. Well, that went well. Often, mentioning that I am Jewish tones down the discussion. Not this man. This pale, grey haired man. The flood gates were open. And he knows because he has friends in Israel. I heard all about those poor Palestinians living there for thousands of years. And the Zionists took over. That the Mosque is on top of two Temples has nothing to do with it. Those evil Jews expelled 800, 000 Palestinians. That it happened because of a war started by 5 Arab states—who cares. And that they lost. What about the 850,000 Jews expelled from Arab countries. Hmm. Don't think he knew that. But, again, so what.

I explained that the Jews are not allowed on the Temple Mount—that is the apartheid in Israel. How dare the Jews go up there! And that Netanyahu—a Nazi. And the Jews are treating the Palestinians like Canada treats its indigenous. Because he knows that Jews are interlopers.

All this coming from an older man, with greying hair, glasses and relatively soft spoken, until he gets to the nitty gritty. Oh, did I mention he doesn't mind Jews—it's those Zionists. Those Nazis. Who would have guessed by looking at him? And his daughter. Look what she is learning.

I eventually lost it. I regret that. But sometimes you have to raise your voice. And I told his lovely daughter do not listen to your father. He is evil. And I called him a racist, a Nazi. An abuse of the word, today.

Nazi no longer carries the Evil within it. It has been used and abused by Holocaust deniers and anyone who is upset on Twitter. And when we accept the equating of Jews with Nazis, what is left?

Despite the fact that I rarely raise my voice in arguments, because I always thought it pointless, I raised mine. Because facts don't matter, today. It is who is the loudest. And not who is right.

What did I learn today? I was reminded about something I have known for a long time. The Jews are the perpetual scapegoat. We are the problem in the world.

But what this man does not know is that we are no longer hiding and ducking and appeasing. No more.

We must raise our voices when we stand next to Evil.

~ Diane Weber Bederman

Published September 5, 2019 – I Saw the Face of Evil Today

https://dianebederman.com/i-saw-the-face-of-evil-today/